INCOME, SAVING, AND
THE THEORY OF CONSUMER BEHAVIOR

Income, Saving, and the Theory of Consumer Behavior

JAMES S. DUESENBERRY

A GALAXY BOOK

New York   OXFORD UNIVERSITY PRESS   1967

To
MY FATHER

PREFACE

THE COMPLETION of this volume will be a relief to my friends who have listened patiently to each new twist in my thinking on the subject. Work on this book began in Washington where I had the benefit of much constructive criticism from Richard Musgrave, Lloyd Metzler, and Alfred Sherrard. In Cambridge I have had much help from Thomas Schelling, William Capron, Carl Kaysen, and Professors Hansen and Leontief. Most of all I am indebted to Evsey Domar and Mary S. Painter, with whom I discussed my difficulties almost every day for six months. Under the title "The Consumption Function" the original version of this book was submitted as a doctoral dissertation at the University of Michigan in February 1948. Acknowledgment is due to W. W. Norton and Company for permission to republish the material in Chapter V which appeared in *Income, Employment and Public Policy; Essays in Honor of Alvin H. Hansen* (1948).

J. S. D.

Cambridge, June 1948

CONTENTS

I. Introduction   1

II. The Empirical Basis of the Theory of Consumers' Choice   6
1. Conceptual schemes and reality. 2. Preference systems and their empirical basis. 3. The independence postulate in utility theory. 4. Conclusion.

III. A Reformulation of the Theory of Saving   17
1. The need for a new departure. 2. Nature of consumption choices. 3. The process of choice. 4. The drive toward higher consumption. 5. The social significance of consumption. 6. Intertemporal choices. 7. Stability of equilibrium. 8 Constancy of the savings ratio. 9. The role of population growth. 10. The distribution of income. 11. Conclusions.

IV. A Theory Versus the Facts   47
1. Income Aspiration and social status. 2. Negro and white savings. 3. Savings and income in individual cities. 4. Long period variations in saving. 5. New consumers' products. 6. Urbanization. 7. The age distribution of the population. 8. Income distribution. 9. The rate of growth of income. 10. Interest rates and expectations. 11. Changes in time preference. 12. Conclusions.

V. Short Run Fluctuations in Saving   69
1. Methods of testing aggregate hypotheses. 2. Saving dependent on past as well as current income. 3. Secular and cyclical movements of the savings ratio.

VI. The Implications of Interdependent Preferences   93
1. Some welfare considerations. 2. The growth of demand.

VII. Conclusions   111
1. Summary. 2. A Qualification. 3. Saving and the business cycle theory.

Bibliography   119

Index   127

TABLES

1. Income and income aspiration   49
2. Relations between the savings ratio and position in the income distribution   54
3. Capital formation and national income by decades, 1879–1938   55
4. Income per consuming unit, proportion saved, and proportion spent on durables, 1879–1928   60
5. Earning ratios of common stocks (per cent)   66
6. Railroad bond yields   66
7. White urban and rural non-farm families with income under $1000 in 1935–36   78
8. Average yearly savings for city families by income change from 1941 to 1942   83
9. Actual and estimated savings as per cent of disposable income   91

CHARTS

I. Saving percentages versus position in income distribution, 1935–36   51
II. Average urban money income and per cent saved, based on surveys of 1901, 1917–1919, 1935–36, and 1941   80

INCOME, SAVING, AND
THE THEORY OF CONSUMER BEHAVIOR

CHAPTER I

INTRODUCTION

IN THE LAST FEW YEARS economists have had to take a somewhat schizophrenic attitude toward the theory of consumption.
In economic theory, analysis ran in terms of preference fields
and utility indices. In business cycles the Keynesian "consumption function" in various forms was used. Most of the work on
the latter concept was empirical and bore little relation to the
theory of consumer behavior. By now, however, Hicks and
others have shown that the Keynesian consumption function is
a special case of the general theory of consumer behavior and
can be deduced from it by making certain assumptions.

This book began as a critique of the Keynesian consumption
function. This critique is based on a demonstration that two
fundamental assumptions of aggregate demand theory are in-
valid. These assumptions are (1) that every individual's consumption behavior is independent of that of every other individual, and (2) that consumption relations are reversible in
time. It is apparent that these two assumptions are just as essential to the general theory of demand as to the consumption
function. Indeed, this must be so since the Keynesian consumption function is a special case of general demand theory.

The connection between the consumption function problem
and the two assumptions just mentioned is readily seen from
empirical considerations. We have three important sets of facts
about the relations between saving and income: (1) the data
on aggregate savings and income in the period 1869–1929 collected by Kuznets; (2) the budget studies of 1935–36 and
1941–42; (3) the yearly data on aggregate savings and income
for the period since 1929 published by the Department of Commerce. The three sets of data are inconsistent if the two hy-

potheses under consideration are accepted. The Kuznets data do not show any tendency for the proportion of income saved to rise with income. The budget study data show that the savings ratio increases with income. The Commerce data also indicate that over the trade cycle the savings ratio varies with income, but the numerical results are not equivalent to those of the budget studies.

Part of the inconsistency is undoubtedly due to errors in the data; but, as we shall show, it is unlikely that errors are sufficient to overcome the difficulty. The inconsistency can also be removed by postulating shifts in the consumption function. But we shall show that the factors usually cited as a basis for trends in consumption are not strong enough to account for the facts. Other factors which could produce trends may exist, of course. On the other hand, there may not be a real inconsistency at all! We have not observed three independent and contradictory measures of the same relation; we have observed three relations among which some connections must exist. Without very much discussion it has been assumed that every individual's consumption is independent of that of every other individual. That implies that (if preferences are uncorrelated with income position) the relation between aggregate income and aggregate consumption can be obtained from a budget study by using weights taken from an income distribution. Because budget studies show that high income groups save a higher proportion of income than low income receivers, it follows that the aggregate savings ratio will rise with income. This contradicts the Kuznets results. Instead of seeking for trend factors we can reëxamine the assumption which leads to the contradiction.

The assumption that each individual's preferences are independent of the behavior of other individuals is fundamental to the general theory of demand as well as to analysis of aggregate savings functions. Consequently, we begin in Chapter II with a reëxamination of the theory of consumer behavior. It is shown there that the indifference map approach to demand theory has an empirical basis. But it is also shown that that basis is inadequate to justify the use of indifference analysis in any argument involving the passage of time. Independence of preferences is necessary for such applications of the indifference approach and there is no empirical basis for that assumption.

In Chapter III it is first shown that there are strong psychological and sociological reasons for supposing that preferences are in fact interdependent. Moreover, it is shown that on certain plausible assumptions we can obtain the following theorem: for any given relative income distribution, the percentage of income saved by a family will tend to be a unique, invariant, and increasing function of its percentile position in the income distribution. The percentage saved will be independent of the absolute level of income. It follows that the aggregate savings ratio will be independent of the absolute level of income. There are, of course, qualifications, which are discussed in Chapter III.

Chapter IV is devoted to empirical tests of the theorem just stated. Some direct tests of the theorem are made. Then the trend factors, such as urbanization, which are supposed to account for upward shifts in the consumption function, are discussed. It is shown that factors of this type operate in both directions, and that their magnitude is insufficient to account for the data.

The theorem stated above is consistent with all the empirical data which are available. It can be easily seen that it removes the inconsistency between Kuznets' data and the budget study data.

We are left with the inconsistency between the annual data on aggregate consumption, which show that the savings ratio varies with income, and the long-period data which indicate that it does not. But that inconsistency is based on the assumption that demand relations are reversible — that is, on the assumption that the change in expenditures resulting from a fall in income is the same in absolute magnitude as that resulting from a rise. In Chapter V it is shown that the reversibility assumption is inconsistent with budget study data. It is argued that, in a depression, the savings ratio can be regarded as a function of the ratio of current income to the highest income previously attained. This is, admittedly, only an approximation, but it seems to work well.

The theorem of Chapter III can now be combined with the one just stated. If in periods of steadily rising income the savings ratio is constant while in depressions the ratio depends on current income and previous peak income, we can explain saving with the relation $S_t / Y_t = 0.25 \, Y_t / Y_o - 0.196$, where S_t and Y_t are current saving and disposable income respectively and Y_o is highest previous disposable income. When fitted to the data, this relation yields a high correlation. Moreover, it accurately predicts the savings rates of 1947.

Many other factors not considered here must influence the rate of saving; for example, asset holdings, interest rates, expectation factors. But the empirical results give strong support to the thesis that the factors discussed here are the dominant ones in the determination of saving.

As I have already indicated, the postulates of independence of preferences and reversibility of demand functions are fundamental to general demand theory. Chapter VI is therefore devoted to a discussion of further implications of the proposition that consumer preferences are interdependent. This assumption has a wide range of applications, two of which are considered in detail. A problem in welfare economics is discussed first. It is well known that on the assumption of independent preferences, income taxes (except on property income) are inconsistent with a conditional maximum of welfare function. This is so because income taxes distort choices between leisure and income.

If we assume instead that preferences are interdependent it can be shown that income taxes are not only consistent with, but *necessary* to a welfare maximum.

In the second part of Chapter VI the interdependence assumption is applied to the problem of demand for new goods. Ordinary demand theory does not give an adequate explanation of the gradual growth in demand for new products. But if we assume that preferences for certain products depend on past rates of sale, a self-generating growth process is set up. It is shown by a simple model that the growth of sales of new products can be explained by such a growth process.

Though only two examples are given here, it can be readily

seen that the assumption of interdependent preferences has a wide range of applications in all fields of demand analysis. Since it provides an adequate explanation of the empirical data on savings, there is a strong case for working out its implications in other fields and testing them there.

CHAPTER II

THE EMPIRICAL BASIS OF THE THEORY OF CONSUMERS' CHOICE

IN MANY DISCUSSIONS of statistical estimation of economic relationships a distinction is made between empirical considerations and *a priori* or theoretical considerations. The latter type of consideration is often used to select the variables to be used in the formal statistical procedure. In the formal consumption literature the theoretical considerations are those derived from the assumption that each individual tries to maximize his utility index. Subject to the limitations imposed by that assumption, the data themselves together with the estimation procedure determine the statistical consumption function. Thus, one part of the procedure is based on strictly empirical considerations, while the other part rests on quite different grounds which are independent of the data used in the statistical analysis.

What is the basis of the distinction between *a priori* and empirical considerations? To what extent are we justified in accepting the limitations imposed by the assumption of utility maximization without an explicit investigation of its empirical validity? We shall show that the "theoretical" considerations themselves have, or anyway ought to have, an empirical basis. Further we shall show that although there is some empirical basis for the utility maximization assumption, that basis is not adequate for the uses to which the assumption is put.

1. CONCEPTUAL SCHEMES AND REALITY

The language of every science involves the use of concepts whose relation to observation is, at best, second hand. If we try to deal directly with observation, we find ourselves faced with an amorphous mass of data which seldom shows any uniformity. We find uniformities only by straining the data through a mesh of artificial concepts. We suppose that uniformities, and simple ones at that, do exist in nature. But nature in the raw is seldom simple because it consists of a large number of separate entities. Each of them may act according to a simple law, but the interaction of all of them taken together is enormously complex.

Essentially we proceed by constructing entities which have not been directly observed, for example, electrons, genes, superegos. These entities are assigned properties sufficient to produce at least some of the data already observed. Having "made up" our concepts we usually find that their properties imply that certain observations not yet considered will occur, under appropriate circumstances. In the experimental sciences the appropriate circumstances are created so as to see whether the predicted observations do occur. If they do, the concept can be accepted for the moment. If they do not, the concept is rejected or at least modified. The history of science is full of instances of concepts which stood up to tests for a while but which were finally rejected, e.g., light-bearing ether, phlogiston, the "humours" of medieval medicine.

The connection of our conceptual entities with observation varies a good deal from one field to another. Probably no one ever expects to observe directly an electron. In other cases the existence of some entity is assumed in order to explain the phenomena. This entity may not yet have been observed but its properties are such that we may hope to observe it if appropriate apparatus can be designed; the gene appears to be in this category. In still other cases we frankly admit that no physical entity exists which corresponds to the concept. This is the case with concepts like that of the superego. The concept is simply a way of thinking. Finally there are cases in which our concepts have directly observable counterparts at the outset. Often, however, we deal with a simplified concept which is supposed to have the "essential" properties of the observable entity. In monetary theory, for example, we have the concept of a commercial bank as a deposit creating and lending organization. Nothing is said about innumerable other aspects of banks because these are not important for our purpose. Thus, even the concepts which have observable counterparts are abstractions from the observations on which they are based. Conceptual schemes are essentially devices for organizing our observation and, in view of their abstract character, it is neither sensible nor important to ask whether they "really" exist.

It seems clear that the choice of a conceptual scheme is somewhat arbitrary. It is probable that a large number of different schemes can be used to "explain" the same observations. That being the case, the validity of a concept depends entirely on the correspondence between the actual observations and those implied by the concept.

We can now see the basis of the distinction between *a priori* considerations and directly empirical ones. Once a concept has been erected and some of its implications tested against available data, it becomes the basis of further theories. By following out all the implications of the concept, we deduce that under certain circumstances certain kinds of events ought to happen and certain others ought not to happen. Suppose we have a theory of consumers' choice which has proved consistent with a mass of observations on consumer behavior. If we seek an explanation of variations in saving we naturally turn to the theory which has proved satisfactory before, and see what it implies with regard to saving. If on application of this procedure a satisfactory explanation is produced, there is no reason to look elsewhere.

If the results are not entirely satisfactory it is still (in view of the previous usefulness of the theory) worth while to try to make minor adjustments in the theory to make it fit the data.

But the value of the latter procedure (as against a basic reformulation of the theory) depends on the success of the theory in explaining other data. In other words, theoretical considerations are fundamentally based on empirical tests but on a broader range of tests than those usually met in estimating a particular statistical relation.

We may now ask what is the empirical basis of the preference system concept which is the basis of the modern theory of consumer behavior. We have first to describe the theory and then to discuss its empirical basis.

2. Preference Systems and their Empirical Basis

The modern theory of consumer behavior grew out of the older marginal utility theory. The latter was based on the propositions (1) that every individual seeks to dispose of his budget in such a way as to maximize total utility, and (2) that the marginal utility of any commodity decreases as its rate of consumption increases.

Inherent in the idea of diminishing marginal utility was the idea of a utility function, that is, of a functional relationship between the quantities of various goods consumed and the utility position of the consumer. In later developments utility as a cardinal magnitude was dropped and the concept of the utility function was replaced by the concept of an ordinal preference field. As Professor Samuelson puts it:[1]

For any two combinations of goods, respectively $(x_1^0, \cdots, x_n^0)$ and $(x_1^1, \cdots, x_n^1)$, or for brevity, X^0 and X^1, it is only necessary that the consumer be able to place them in one of the following mutually exclusive categories:

a. (X^0) preferred to (X^1)
b. (X^1) preferred to (X^0)
c. (X^0) and (X^1) equally preferred or indifferent.

For convenience, we may attach a number to each combination; this is assumed to be a continuous differentiable function. This function (or rule of numbering) may be written

$$\varphi = \varphi(X) = \varphi(x_1, \cdots, x_n).$$

It is so constructed that the following three conditions correspond to the above three respectively:

a'. $\varphi(X^1) < \varphi(X^0)$
b'. $\varphi(X^0) < \varphi(X^1)$
c'. $\varphi(X^0) = \varphi(X^1).$

φ may be designated as a utility index.

[1] Paul A. Samuelson, *Foundations of Economic Analysis* (Cambridge, Mass.: Harvard University Press, 1947), p. 94.

Once the concept of a utility index is developed, it can be shown that if the consumer chooses goods in such a way as to maximize the utility index (subject to the constraint that the value of his purchases cannot exceed his income), his actions will be determinate. That is, the only variables relevant to the determination of consumer purchases are prices and income. It can further be shown that the demand functions are homogeneous of zero order, that is, they are unaffected by proportional changes in all prices and income. Certain other theorems can be derived, but not the shape or sign of simple derivatives of demand functions.

The concept of the preference field can be extended so that choices with regard to consumption at different times are taken into account. It can then be shown that the consumer's action at any moment depends on his assets, his current and expected future income, and current and expected future prices and interest rates. The homogeneity postulate now applies to all the variables (except interest rates), unless uncertainty is introduced when it disappears altogether. The shape of the demand functions remains undetermined.

All this appears to be intuitively acceptable and moderately useful. It is useful in two ways. If we are well enough informed about particular markets we may be able to make some judgments which enable us to guess the shape of certain demand functions. We can then make qualitative estimates of the effects of changes in some of the parameters either on the supply side or in the preferences themselves. Marshall regarded such judgments as possible for that "well-informed citizen" who appears so often in his pages.

If we are not sufficiently well informed to make such judgments, we can use the results of the preference analysis as the basis for statistical work. The preference analysis gives us a list of relevant variables. This leaves us the problem of choosing the functional forms to be used; a problem which can often be solved by the use of approximations which will hold good for certain ranges of the data. The remaining task of estimating numerical parameters is one of data collection and statistical technique.

But if we are to use preference functions for such important purposes, can we let the case rest on its intuitive acceptability?

In attempting to get beyond intuition we can begin by asking what kind of experiment could be set up to test whether satisfactory preference fields exist. It is extraordinarily difficult to design experiments of the right sort which could in fact be carried out. But, for purposes of elucidating the meaning of the preference system concept, we may conceive of experiments which are technically impractical.

Imagine then that we have an experimental subject who has given current income and assets and given expectations about future income, prices, and interest rates. Further, over the period of the experiment, the subject is effectively isolated from all influences which might change his expectations or produce autonomous changes in his tastes. We now offer the subject a variety of commodities at certain prices. Suppose for example that our subject is a housewife about to buy a week's groceries. The subject decides what to buy and the decisions are recorded. (The subject must of course believe that the transactions are genuine.) Now let us suppose that we are able to bring the customer back to the initial position and repeat the experiment with a different set of prices. Presumably we should have to administer a drug which would make the subject forget the events of the experiment. Assuming that this can be accomplished, we could repeat the experiment a number of times and thus turn out a section of the subject's preference field.

If we could make such experiments, what results would lead us to decide that the preference field concept was unsatisfactory? First, we would be dissatisfied with the concept if the experimental results revealed inconsistencies in preferences. If combination A is preferred to combination B, and B to C, then C should not be preferred to A. If inconsistency in preferences is general, then we cannot say that choices are determined by income and prices alone. Minor inconsistencies can be tolerated, of course. No significant adjustments in the theory need be made if it can be maintained that the frequency of inconsistencies grows smaller as the differences among the alternatives become greater.

Secondly, we should be dissatisfied if behavior appeared to be capricious or random. Suppose we offered the same prices a large number of times and found that the combinations purchased were distributed equally among the possible alternatives. If this were the case, we should only know that the consumer could not spend more than his whole income. In this case the effects of price or income changes would be the same regardless of the shape of preference functions and the concept would have to be abandoned as an aid in the explanation of saving.

This objection would not apply if behavior contained a random component but had a strong central tendency. In this case statements about individual demand would have to be probabilistic, but little modification in the theory of market demand would be required.

We cannot carry out the experiments just described, but all of us use introspection to reach a conclusion as to the importance of inconsistency and randomness in behavior. So much has been written on the question that it would be superfluous to argue out the case here. It seems safe to say that it is the judgment of most who have considered the question, that the preference system is not invalidated either by inconsistencies in preferences or capriciousness in consumer behavior. Certainly consumers do act inconsistently and impulsively to some extent. But few want to maintain that preferences are not sufficiently definite to dominate behavior.

Our introspective estimate of the results of the experiment just described tells us that *at every moment* we have a well ordered system of preferences. Moreover, we feel that if we were subject to no outside influences and remained in the same objective situation, our preferences would remain unchanged.[2]

Our evidence on this question is not confined to introspection. Each of us is equipped with a body of observations on the behavior of other people which confirms the idea that everyone

---

[2] Of course particular individuals cannot stay in the same situation indefinitely because they are growing older. If, however, no autonomous forces are at work, there is no reason to suppose that the mere passage of time as such would make one generation's preferences (on the average) different from those of another.

has a well-ordered preference system at every moment. Moreover, we can confirm our interpretation of overt behavior by discussing tastes and differences in tastes. There is enough information to confirm us in our belief that the concept of a preference field is a meaningful one. Thus the utility theory, in its modern form at any rate, is not merely a remnant of an outmoded psychological theory as some have maintained, but has an empirical basis.

But the scope of these observations on which the preference theory is based is rather limited. However, it is sufficient to demonstrate the existence of well-ordered preferences at any particular moment. But if we tried to base economic theory on so limited a proposition we would not get very far. In practice, preference systems have been used in a way which assumes much more than the existence of preferences at every moment. For a long time it has been assumed that "tastes" can be regarded as part of the data of economics. That does not mean that tastes are constant in time. But it does mean that the parameters of preference systems are substantially independent of the other economic variables. In particular it usually implies that the preferences of each individual are independent of the actual purchases of others. Otherwise it would be impossible to obtain aggregate demand curves by the simple addition of individual demands.

There is little observational warrant for the independence of different individuals' preferences yet it is implicit in most economic theory. The assumption has slipped in during the course of the historical development of consumer behavior theory.

3. THE INDEPENDENCE POSTULATE IN UTILITY THEORY

In the early stages of the development of utility theory attention was centered on the demonstration of the important role played by utility in the determination of value. The early utility theorists were not only concerned with the development of their own theory; they had to attack and overcome the well-entrenched cost theory which had dominated economic thinking for nearly a century. Perhaps for this reason they were primarily concerned with the demonstration of existence theorems. None of the originators of the utility theory gives any extended discussion of changes in preferences.

Marshall clearly believed that preferences do in fact change with time. In keeping with his general point of view he supposes that wants are continuously evolving as a result of the development of new activities. But the discussion of wants and activities is divorced from the discussion of the utility theory and from the analysis of markets. He does, of course, give a warning that it takes time for equilibria to work out and that the data (including tastes) may change before the equilibrium is reached. Marshall believed that this difficulty could be overcome by the use of his time period analysis. It is probably true that a skilled practitioner could avoid the problems posed by changing data through the use of Marshallian methods. But the real difficulty lies deeper. Are we justified in taking tastes as data at all? Are changes in tastes due to autonomous factors or are they (at least partly) due to economic events? In particular are the preferences of one individual affected by the actual behavior of others? If that is so, the preference systems in existence at one moment are the consequence of actual purchases in the past. We cannot say that our problem is to find how the system adapts to the data if the data are changing with the adaptation.

The interdependence of preference systems has been recognized since the earliest days of economics. One can find discussions of emulation and the desire for distinction in the non-analytic parts of Jevons and Marshall, not to mention such writers as Veblen and Frank Knight. But, in Jevons and Marshall, remarks on this subject are mere *obiter dicta* and do not affect the formal analysis.[3] Writers like Knight and Veblen on the other hand were engaged in criticism of the neo-classical economics. Veblen attacked analytical economics and tried to substitute for it a historical approach. For the most part his work bears on questions different from those dealt with in analytical economics and, whatever its other merits, throws

---

[3] But see Pigou, "Some Remarks on Utility," *Economic Journal,* vol. 13 (1903).

little light on problems of resource allocation and employment. Knight's critiques on utility theory were written primarily in connection with a discussion of the relations of economics and ethics.

Both Veblen and Knight made real contributions to our understanding of consumer behavior problems. But because their interest lay in other fields they did not try to develop a positive analytical theory of consumption — one which would take into account the interdependence of preferences and still be useful in connection with the problems traditionally called economic. The negative character of their comments on "orthodox" demand theory explains, in large measure, their lack of influence on it. Most people would rather have a bad theory than no theory at all.

Orthodoxy has another defense. Everyone agrees that science must proceed by abstraction. We must center our attention on a relatively small number of important determinants of behavior and neglect the rest lest we be lost in a sea of facts. The utility theory and its derivatives are supposed to take into account the important factors in consumer behavior. Anyone who insists on bringing in other elements can easily be regarded as a naive realist in the same class with those people who argue from particular instances which contradict statistical results. This charge can only be answered by a demonstration of the quantitative importance of the interdependence of preferences.

4. CONCLUSION

So far we have shown (1) that so-called *a priori* considerations actually require an empirical basis, (2) that the modern theory of consumer choice has an empirical basis, but (3) there is no empirical justification for the implicit assumptions underlying the application of the preference system analysis. Finally we have suggested that criticism of the preference system analysis has failed to influence the development of economic theory. It appears that this failure is due to the failure of the critics to prove empirically the importance of interdependence or to offer any substitute for the analytic scheme provided by the preference system concept.

It might seem logical to begin by proving the importance of interdependence and then proceed to develop an analytic framework for dealing with it. It will be convenient, however, to proceed in the opposite way. The next chapter is devoted to a development of a theory of saving which takes into account the interdependence of preferences. Chapter IV is an attempt to kill two birds with one stone. We try to show that, on the one hand, the saving theory of Chapter III is consistent with the data and, on the other, the alternative hypothesis is not. The inconsistencies in the data which are removed by the interdependence assumption are of such importance that this factor cannot any longer be written off as a minor one.

CHAPTER III

A REFORMULATION OF THE THEORY OF SAVING

1. THE NEED FOR A NEW DEPARTURE

THE PREFERENCE system analysis of consumer behavior is a somewhat remarkable tour de force. It seems to say something about consumer behavior without saying anything about the motivations of the consumers in question. In its present form it is a more or less deliberate attempt to sidestep the task of making any psychological assumptions. It has the advantage that it allows one to avoid getting out on a psychological limb which may collapse at any moment. Moreover, if no changes in taste except autonomous ones occurred, the preference system scheme would serve its purpose. But, if tastes are interdependent, a dynamic development in tastes is implied. Analysis of the dynamics of tastes requires an analysis of the driving forces in the development.

In a purely formal way we could continue to use the preference analysis. We could make the parameters of preference functions dependent on the past sales of products. In Chapter VI this type of argument is applied to the analysis of the growth of demand for new products. At a certain stage that type of analysis may be useful. But until a well-developed general demand theory is available, analysis in terms of shifting preferences is a little difficult. We find ourselves in the position of analyzing phenomena in terms of changes in an unobservable parameter. Ordinarily we try to measure preference parameters (or functions of them) by market behavior, since we cannot observe the preferences directly. With shifting parameters we should be carrying indirect measurement a step farther. We would not only have to measure the preference parameters but the parameters of the relation governing shifts in the preferences. Neither set of parameters can be observed directly. If we consider that both sets are subject to autonomous changes it must be agreed that empirical analysis in terms of shifting parameters would be impossible.

Another approach would be the use of generalized preference systems. We can suppose that each individual has an ordered set of preferences, not only for different combinations of goods for himself, but for different combinations of goods for himself and other people. A formal analysis in terms of such generalized preference functions could certainly be constructed. But to get any useful results — to impose any restrictions on demand functions — we should have to specify something about the shape of the preference functions. To do that it is necessary to introduce psychological postulates going beyond those of simple preference functions.

In short, we have to face up to the problems of the psychological bases of consumer choice. But as soon as one considers that problem one sees why economists have tried to avoid it. At first glance every conceivable motivation seems to be involved in consumer choices. If we wish to explain in detail every purchase by every individual we are in a hopeless position. We certainly cannot create a useful analytical scheme on the basis of detailed individual psychology.

This consideration need not detain us very long. We are, after all, primarily concerned with the central tendencies of the relations between economic variables and consumer choices. If it can be shown that one set of forces dominates the behavior of most individuals, we can center our attention on the operation of those forces. The other variables will produce certain unexplained residuals. But if these are sufficiently small we may neglect them.

At this point we can see the difference between our solution to the problem of motivation and that of the preference system analysts. The latter wished to have a completely general theory which could (at least formally) take into account every individual psychological variation and every force impinging on choices. At the same time they could not produce a psychological theory adequate to that task. Their solution is a preference system for every individual. Psychological differences (as well as differences in other circumstances) between individuals are handled by giving different individuals different preference systems. Any factors which change their decisions (in given economic conditions) can be represented by autonomous changes in the preference parameters. Thus the analysis is perfectly general and explains every detail of consumption behavior. Yet no psychological commitments have been made. But, as we have shown, this ingenious solution breaks down if the preferences are interdependent.

We are faced with the same problem. We do not want to analyze every impulse affecting consumption decisions any more than anyone else. We try to solve the problem by being less ambitious. Instead of explaining every detail of consumption behavior, we try to explain the average behavior of a large group. Secondly, we are less wary. We shall make some definite commitments of a psychological and sociological nature. We may be wrong about them so that we take a certain risk which the preference system analysts avoided. On the other hand we are compensated by being able to deal with the interdependence problem and by getting more definite results than can be obtained from the preference analysis.

In this chapter a new theory of saving is developed. By showing that a theory of saving based on the interdependence of preferences explains the facts about saving, we demonstrate the importance of interdependence. At the same time we lay the groundwork for a general theory of consumer choice.

2. NATURE OF CONSUMPTION CHOICES

A real understanding of the problem of consumer behavior must begin with a full recognition of the social character of consumption patterns. From the viewpoint of preference theory or marginal utility theory, human desires are desires for specific goods; but nothing is said about how these desires arise or how they are changed. That, however, is the essence of the consumption problem when preferences are interdependent.

If we ask why consumers desire the things they buy, we raise a problem which has to be dealt with on several different levels.

We know, of course, that certain goods are purchased to maintain physical existence or physical comfort. We also know that certain activities are an essential part of our culture, or, at least, of parts of it. Some of these activities, for example, traveling to work, are accessory to acquisition of goods used for other purposes. Others are required to maintain social status. Still others are undertaken merely for pleasure. But in every case the kinds of activities in which people engage are culturally determined and constitute only a small subset of the possible actions in which people might participate. Nearly all purchases of goods are made, ostensibly at least, either to provide physical comfort or to implement the activities which make up the life of our culture. Frequently, of course, both kinds of requirement are satisfied by the same goods.

All this is so obvious that it hardly seems worth while to dwell on it. Yet it is vitally important for the present theory. For we can now argue that people do not, for the most part, desire specific goods but desire goods which will serve certain purposes.

But, of course, people are not indifferent as between the goods which will serve the same purpose. People who want transportation care whether they walk or ride a subway or in a taxi. Almost any activity can be carried out in a variety of ways and a variety of goods can be used to implement it. Sometimes the goods which can be substituted for one another for a single purpose go by different names, as in the transportation case; sometimes they are different brands or varieties of the same kind of goods. But the important point is that they are qualitatively different ways of doing the same thing. Even more important they are not just different but some are better than others.

The superiority of one good over another for a specific purpose may be a technical superiority, as in the case of automobiles or refrigerators. In other cases it may be an aesthetic superiority or superiority with respect to some criterion such as newness of design. But whatever the basis of the comparison there is likely to be, at one time, a high degree of agreement about the best means of satisfying any particular need. This agreement will be particularly strong in the fields of food, housing, household operation, clothing, and transportation, which absorb the largest part of most family budgets. Whether the agreement arises because of the objective differences in the goods in question or because of advertising or the prestige of fashion leaders need not concern us particularly at the moment. There will, of course, be plenty of disagreements about the merits of specific items. But, if a large number of people were asked to rank, in order of preference, a number of different types of automobiles, houses, or cuts of meat, the rank correlation would be high. This would be particularly true if the whole range of substitutes from the cheapest to the most expensive were included. Of course, the correlation obtained in this kind of test would be higher the more homogeneous the group involved. Age differences, regional differences, and differences in social class will reduce the correlation. But the correlation would still be quite high even if a random sample of the whole population were used. The lowest correlation would presumably result from a test of agreement on aesthetic or recreational activities; but these items account for a small part of most budgets, even in high income groups.

So far all our emphasis has been upon qualitative differences. But, of course, quantitative variations are also important. Variation in the quantities of goods consumed has a number of different aspects. In some cases quantitative variation is variation in the proportion of times in which one or another of a set of substitutes is used for a given purpose. A man may eat dinner every night, sometimes in an expensive restaurant, sometimes in a cheap one. If he increases the proportion of times in which he eats in the expensive one, then he is, in a sense, improving the average quality of his meals.

In a second group of situations quantity differences are essentially differences in variety. The quality of a library depends on the number of books not because more books fill up more space but because the books are different. Quantity is also associated with specialization. A woman wants a large stock of dresses, not only for variety, but because some are evening dresses and some afternoon dresses, etc. If she owns only a few she is doomed to wear the same dress for different purposes.

When goods are looked at as the means of carrying out activities, their quality clearly varies with the degree to which they are specialized to suit specific purposes.

There are, of course, cases in which quantity variations are directly important. It is presumably better to have a large steak than a small one. But for our purposes there is no difficulty in looking at this as a special case of quality variation.

On the whole it appears safe to build a theory of consumption around the four propositions: (1) physical needs and the activities required by the culture require the consumption of certain kinds of goods; and (2) each of the needs, whether physically or socially generated, can be satisfied by any of a number of qualitatively different types of goods; (3) these different types of goods, or, in the broader sense, ways of doing things, are regarded as superior or inferior to one another; (4) there is a generally agreed-upon scale of ranks for the goods which can be used for any specific purpose.

Nothing that has been said so far is formally inconsistent with the use of preference theory or utility theory. These approaches emphasize changes in the quantities of a set of goods. Formally these approaches are more general. But they lead one to think of differences in consumption patterns in terms of differences in the amounts of the same specific goods rather than in terms of the qualities of goods consumed. But it seems clear that psychologically an improvement in the living standard consists in satisfying one's needs in a better way. This may sometimes involve consuming more of something but it very often consists in consuming something different. In what follows we shall find the quality approach to consumption a useful tool.

3. The Process of Choice

The level of saving actually achieved by anyone represents the outcome of the conflict between his desire to improve his current standard of living and his desire to obtain future welfare by saving. To understand the way in which the outcome of the struggle is determined, we need to know something about the motivations leading toward increased expenditure and those which make saving desirable. To begin with, however, we need a picture of the consumer in action. For this purpose we need only the most general ideas about motivation. On the one hand we can simply assume for the moment that people wish to save for some reason. The motivations behind saving are discussed in detail in section 6. On the consumption side it may be assumed that in choosing consumption goods everyone will always prefer higher quality goods to lower quality goods. But usually superior goods will be more expensive (superiority here being regarded as a subjective not as an objective matter). Inferior goods which are expensive will not be sold and can be eliminated from consideration. That implies that, with a given income, one can improve the quality of one's living standard only by reducing saving.

In preference theory and marginal utility theory the consumer is supposed to consider a sort of menu showing all of the available goods and services and their prices. He then decides how much to consume of each. No one believes that this actually happens. But it can be argued that consumers make the same decisions as they would if they went through a systematic budgeting procedure. This is possible, though extremely doubtful. In any case it will be worth while to see if any new elements appear when we make a more realistic description of the way in which consumer decisions are actually made.

We have already concluded that people use goods and services in order to satisfy certain needs or to carry out certain activities. The physical needs are a given datum and for our purposes most of the activities carried on by an individual can be predicted if we know his age, occupation, social status, and marital status. (Specific recreational activities are an exception here but not a very important one.) On the whole then, the consumer has only one degree of freedom in making choices about consumption. *He can vary the quality of the goods and services he uses for any purpose.*

Whenever it is necessary to acquire goods or services, for any of the purposes we have discussed, a decision has to be made as to the quality of goods to be purchased. These decisions are not made simultaneously, but individually, as the necessity for a particular purchase arises. This might seem to imply that the decisions are made independently of one another, but that is only partly true. The decisions have to be related because of the budget constraint and the desire to save. But the mechanism which connects consumption decisions is not that of rational planning but of learning and habit formation.

The process of habit formation is difficult to describe in a short space because it is a genetic process which begins in childhood. At any one moment a consumer already has a well-established set of consumption habits. However, the central elements in the process can be brought out by a hypothetical example of a forced change in habits.

Suppose a man suffers a 50 per cent reduction in his income and expects this reduction to be permanent. Immediately after the change he will tend to act in the same way as before. When the situations which led him to make expenditures before recur, he will continue to respond by making the same expenditures. But if he does this for a time he will find that his assets are being reduced; or if he had none he will find that late in the income period he has to forego purchases which seem more important than those made earlier. In retrospect he will regret some of his expenditures. In the ensuing periods the same stimuli as before will arise, but eventually he will learn to reject some expenditures and respond by buying cheap substitutes for the goods formerly purchased. Eventually he will reach a new consumption pattern such that he will not, in retrospect, regret any of his expenditures. This pattern is likely to become habitual in the same way as the original pattern.

This is, of course, a very oversimplified description of what must be an extremely complicated process. An economist will note at once that the behavior just described did not involve any rational planning. Actually, of course, a man faced with a reduction in income may decide in advance to change his consumption pattern. But this does not change any essential elements in the process. Such planning results from the ability of men to imagine that an action will have undesirable results. Instead of discovering the unfortunate results of some kind of behavior by an actual experiment, we do so by a mental experiment. From a learning theory standpoint this is the central difference between mice and men.

The elements in the consumption habit formation process are (1) the basic physical or social needs which can be satisfied by the acquisition of goods or services; (2) experimental behavior (real or imaginary); (3) the results of this behavior, that is, in some cases regret that certain expenditures were made; (4) learning that a certain pattern is successful in the sense that no expenditures are regretted to a sufficient extent to cause a change in the pattern.

4. THE DRIVE TOWARD HIGHER CONSUMPTION

We have already said that our problem is to explain the resolution of a conflict — the struggle between desires to increase expenditure and desires to save or balance the budget. To do this we have to discover the nature of the forces on both sides. Here we consider the forces leading to higher consumption expenditures.

In the last section we simply assumed that everyone wants to improve the quality of the goods he uses for any purpose. Granting the fact, what is the source of this drive?

Of course, quality was defined in terms of preference so that there must be some desire to get high quality goods or there would be no preference. But we now have to find the source of a drive sufficiently strong to account for the amount of work people do, and for the small size of their savings in the face of considerable insecurity. Since some goods are used to satisfy physical needs one might argue that the drive to improve their quality depends on their relative effectiveness in satisfying physical needs. Similarly, other goods are used to implement culturally determined activities. One might suppose that the drive to spend more on these goods stems from the superior "effectiveness" of some goods — effectiveness being judged in terms of comfort, convenience, beauty, or whatever else is relevant.

That the problem is not so simple is shown by the fact that in many societies people are unwilling to make sacrifices to improve the quality of their consumption in terms of the criteria just mentioned. Our own society furnishes further evidence. Thirty years ago the average urban family with a $1500 income in 1940 prices saved 8 per cent of its income. In 1941 a similarly placed family saved nothing. One can hardly argue that the desire for saving, whatever its source, had diminished in that period. For some reason, the forces leading to higher consumption increased during that period, and it is difficult to attribute that increase to biological changes or changes in sensitivity to considerations of comfort or convenience.

In a fundamental sense the basic source of the drive toward higher consumption is to be found in the character of our culture. A rising standard of living is one of the major goals of our society. Much of our public policy is directed toward this end. Societies are compared with one another on the basis of the size of their incomes. In the individual sphere people do not expect to live as their parents did, but more comfortably and conveniently. The consumption pattern of the moment is conceived of not as part of a way of life, but only as a temporary adjustment to circumstances. We expect to take the first available chance to change the pattern. In view of this attitude it is easy to see why consumption will increase with income. But we have raised a more difficult question. What makes people with a given income increase their consumption?

In the last section we considered the problem of consumer choice in terms of habit formation. A family in given circumstances manages to achieve a *modus operandi* between its desires for increased consumption and its desires for saving. The solution, whatever it is, is a compromise. The family knows of the existence of higher quality goods and would prefer them to the ones now in use. But it could only attain these by giving up saving. Once a compromise is reached the habit formation provides a protective wall against desires for higher quality goods. In given circumstances, the individuals in question come into contact with goods superior to the ones they use with a certain frequency. Each such contact is a demonstration of the superiority of these goods and is a threat to the existence of the current consumption pattern. It is a threat because it makes active the latent preference for these goods. A certain effort is required to resist the impulse to give up saving in favor of higher quality goods. (This resistance need not, of course, be entirely conscious, but psychic effort is required all the same.)

Suppose the consumption patterns of other people are given. Consumption expenditures of a particular consumer will have to rise until the frequency of contact with superior goods is reduced to a certain level. This level of frequency has to be sufficiently low to permit resistance to all impulses to increase expenditures. The strength of the resistance will depend on the strength of desires for saving.

It now becomes clear how the habit pattern can be broken without a change in income or prices. For any particular family the frequency of contact with superior goods will increase primarily as the consumption expenditures of others increase. When that occurs, impulses to increase expenditure will increase in frequency, and strength and resistance to them will be inadequate. The result will be an increase in expenditure at the expense of saving.

We might call this the "demonstration effect." People believe that the consumption of high quality goods for any purpose is desirable and important. If they habitually use one set of goods, they can be made dissatisfied with them by a demonstration of the superiority of others. But mere knowledge of the existence of superior goods is not a very effective habit breaker. Frequent contact with them may be. In this field it is not only true that "what you don't know won't hurt you," but that what you do know does hurt you.

The best way to demonstrate that consumption expenditures can be forced up by contact with superior goods is to ask the reader to consult his own experience. What kind of reaction is produced by looking at a friend's new car or looking at houses or apartments better than one's own? The response is likely to be a feeling of dissatisfaction with one's own house or car. If this feeling is produced often enough it will lead to action which eliminates it, that is, to an increase in expenditure.

We can maintain then that the frequency and strength of impulses to increase expenditure depends on frequency of contact with goods superior to those habitually consumed. This effect need not depend at all on considerations of emulation or "conspicuous consumption."

5. THE SOCIAL SIGNIFICANCE OF CONSUMPTION

So far it has been assumed that impulses to increase expenditure arise only out of a belief in the superiority of certain goods for fulfilling some need. But there is another aspect of consumption which is perhaps equally important. Ours is a society in which one of the principal social goals is a higher standard of living. Now the fact that the attainment of a higher standard of living as an end in itself is a major social goal has great significance for the theory of consumption. For this means that the desire to get superior goods takes on a life of its own. It provides a drive to higher expenditure which may be even stronger than that arising out of the needs which are supposed to be satisfied by the expenditure.

The mechanism may be described in the following way. When the attainment of any end becomes a generally recognized social goal, the importance of attainment of this goal is instilled in every individual's mind by the socialization process. In psychoanalytic terms the goal is incorporated into the ego-ideal. When this occurs the achievement of a certain degree of success in reaching the goal becomes essential to the maintenance of self-esteem. The maintenance of self-esteem is a basic drive in every individual.[1] Indeed, many psychological problems involve conflict between the requirements of self-esteem, for example, the attainment of some goal or the maintenance of some prohibition, on the one hand, and the requirements of some other drive on the other. We do not have to

[1] Cf. K. Horney, *The Neurotic Personality of Our Time* (New York: W. W. Norton & Company, Inc., 1937). The view that a great deal of human behavior can be explained on the basis of considerations of prestige or maintenance of self-esteem is also supported by recent experimental work on levels of aspirations. It has been shown, for example, that in intelligence tests the level of performance desired by a subject as well as his actual performance is influenced by comparing his performance on past tests favorably or unfavorably with groups whom the subject regards as superior or inferior to himself in intelligence. See L. Festinger, "Wish, Expectation and Group Standards as Factors Influencing Level of Aspiration," *Journal of Abnormal and Social Psychology*, vol. 37 (January 1942).

question the existence of the drive to maintain self-esteem, but only the kind of activity which it requires. It seems fairly obvious that improvement in the standard of living is identical with improvement in the quality of goods consumed. In a society in which improvement in the living standard is a social goal, the drive for maintenance of self-esteem will become a drive to get higher quality goods. It can operate quite independently of the desirability of these goods from any other standpoint.

It is well known that there are societies in which prestige is gained by the acquisition of some sort of good which is completely useless in fulfilling any need whatever. In spite of the complete uselessness of the things in question, their acquisition may be vital to the acquisition of prestige or maintenance of self-esteem. A great deal of effort may be expended in acquiring these useless items.[2] In our society people may think that they expend effort to get a Buick instead of a Chevrolet because the Buick is more comfortable or goes faster. But this does not in the least prove that part of the basis for the purchase is not the maintenance of self-esteem.

The force of the drive toward higher living standards — that is, toward the purchase of superior goods — is greatly strengthened in our society by the characteristics of our social structure. Ours is a society, which is formally classless, but which is nevertheless characterized by a system of differentiated social status.

There are a number of criteria for attainment of relatively high status of which the most important appear to be occupational success (which in most cases means, or at least is accompanied by, high income), membership in occupational groups of relatively high prestige, and family connections. The last factor is probably of major importance only in small communities or among individuals of extremely high status. Attainment of a given status also requires an ability to meet the behavioral standards of other members of high status groups. Thus, it is possible for some individuals with low incomes to maintain a very high status while others with very high incomes may fail

[2] Cora Dubois, *The People of Alor* (Minneapolis: University of Minnesota Press, 1944), p. 23.

to achieve the highest positions. In general, however, it appears that income is one of the principal status criteria. Prestige goes to successful people and success in our society is closely correlated with income. Once a group of high income people are recognized as a group of superior status, their consumption standard itself becomes one of the criteria for judging success. Since almost any consumption theory is consistent with the view that high-income families will spend more on consumption than low-income families, high standards of consumption become established as criteria for high status. Once this has occurred, it becomes difficult for anyone to attain a high status position unless he can maintain a high consumption standard, regardless of any other qualifications he may have.[3]

Further force is given to the drive toward high consumption standards by the high degree of social mobility possible in our society. In a society in which the criteria for status are in terms of birth it is impossible for an individual to raise his status. Therefore, the drive to attain a high standard of consumption as a means to attaining high status is blunted.[4]

Moreover, our society is not stratified; that is, it does not maintain any strong barriers against association among individuals of different status. This means that the frequency with which an individual can make invidious comparisons between the quality of his living standard and that of others is greatly increased. Of course, almost by definition, the existence of social status means that every individual tends to associate with other individuals of nearly the same status. But since social status rankings in our society form a continuous series[5] rather than a set of clearly defined group rankings, every individual must associate with some people of higher or lower status than his own. Of necessity then, in view of our social goals, every individual makes comparisons between his own living standard and those of his associates in higher or

---

[3] Cf. W. L. Warner, *The Social Life of a Modern Community* (New Haven: Yale University Press, 1941), pp. 85–91; G. W. Hartman, "The Prestige of Occupations," *Personnel Journal*, XIII, 144–152; R. B. Cattell, "The Concept of Social Status," *Journal of Social Psychology*, XV (May 1942), 293–307.

[4] Warner, *loc. cit.*

[5] Warner, *loc. cit.*

lower status positions. Every unfavorable comparison of this sort leads to an impulse to buy goods which will raise the quality of the living standard, and eliminate the unfavorable comparison.[6]

Our social goal of a high standard of living, then, converts the drive for self-esteem into a drive to get high quality goods. The possibility of social mobility and recognition of upward mobility as a social goal converts the drive for self-esteem into a desire for high social status. But since high social status requires the maintenance of a high consumption standard, the drive is again converted into a drive to obtain high quality goods. In both cases the drive operates through inferiority feelings aroused by unfavorable comparisons between living standards. The strength of such feelings suffered by one individual varies with the frequency with which he has to make an unfavorable comparison between the quality of the goods he uses with those used by others. This frequency will depend, as we have already shown, on the ratio of his expenditures to those of others with whom he comes into contact.

[6] The interconnections between self-esteem and the social status system are clearly set forth by Kardiner. He says, "Despite political equality, a hierarchy of social prestige values exists in the status-class-prestige system which is so pervasive that no one can ignore it. Social mobility theoretically permits the individual to move from one class to another. This produces a background against which the self-esteem of the individual is always reflected. A high degree of competitiveness exists, therefore, about status-class-prestige values, though no such rivalry appears with regard to subsistence." — "The comparative liquidity of status class causes the greatest instability because the life goals of the individual must be polarized toward the goal of success as form of self-validation." A. Kardiner, *The Psychological Frontiers of Society* (New York: Columbia University Press, 1945), p. 341.

"The anxieties of Western man are, therefore, concerned with success as a form of self-realization in the same way that salvation was in the Middle Ages. But in comparison with the individual who merely sought salvation, the psychological task for modern man is much more arduous. It is a responsibility, and failure brings with it less social censure and contempt than it does self-contempt, a feeling of inferiority and hopelessness. Success is a goal without satiation point, and the desire for it, instead of abating, increases with achievement. The use made of success is largely power over others, since the advantages in the form of luxurious types of subsistence, 'conspicuous waste,' are easily exhausted. Those who have power or wealth set the fashion for all others to imitate, and social mobility is interpreted largely as the achievement of more success, to improve the standard of living, to ape the manners of those who are rich, and to have the gratification of having some 'power' too" (p. 445).

In view of these considerations it seems quite possible that after some minimum income is reached, the frequency and strength of impulses to increase expenditures for one individual depend entirely on the ratio of his expenditures to the expenditures of those with whom he associates. It will not be possible to give a conclusive proof of this hypothesis, but it will be possible to show that it provides a very plausible working hypothesis. For this reason it seems desirable to work out the full implications of the hypothesis. To do this it will be necessary to find a basis by means of which the forces leading to impulses to spend can be compared with those leading to the rejection of these impulses.

The analysis of the forces causing impulses to consume shows that these arise when an individual makes an unfavorable comparison of his living standard with that of someone else. If these impulses must be rejected, the individual is dissatisfied with his position. For one consumer, the number and strength of impulses to consume *more* depends on the ratio of his expenditures to expenditures by other individuals. Dissatisfaction arises from the rejection of impulses to spend. Consequently the dissatisfaction with his consumption standard which an individual must undergo is a function of the ratio of his expenditures to those of people with whom he associates.

Thus if C_i is the consumption expenditure of one individual and U_i is his utility index, we may write $U_i = U_i[C_i/\Sigma\alpha_{ij}C_j]$ where C_j is consumption of the jth individual and α_{ij} is the weight applied by the ith consumer to the expenditure of the jth. This, of course, only tells how the utility index varies with respect to current consumption. We must now consider how it varies with respect to saving.

6. INTERTEMPORAL CHOICES

The traditional theory of saving is part of the general theory of consumers' choice. As such it involves two distinct elements: the preferences of the consumer and the objective situations with which he is faced. In its most general form the theory states:

(1) That a consumer's utility index is a function of his consumption and asset holdings at various points in time;

(2) That at the decision point he has a certain current income and asset position;

(3) That at the decision point he has certain expectations about future non-interest income;

(4) That he is faced with a certain current interest rate and certain expectations about future rates;

(5) That the consumer will act in such a way as to get on to the highest indifference surface permitted by the conditions (2), (3), and (4).

This theory is a perfectly general one provided that the preferences are consistent and behavior is not capricious. In particular it does not involve any assertion to the effect that people save for "rational" reasons, that is, to retire, provide for contingencies, etc. If people save from habit or because they like to look at their bank books, that is perfectly consistent with the theory. So far so good. But how is the theory to be modified to take into acount the interdependence of choices discussed in the last section?

We can safely assume that a consumer's choices between present and future are not strongly affected *directly* by the actions of other people. Most people do not know how much their neighbors save or what their assets are. Consequently they cannot be directly affected by other people's saving decisions. Our critique of preference analysis on grounds of interdependence does not apply in this connection.

But choices between present and future consumption will be indirectly affected by the interdependence of desires for current consumption. Suppose a man's desires for current consumption were increased by increases in other people's consumption while his desires for future consumption were not. Then increases in other people's consumption would twist his present-future indifference curves. At any given point on the map he would trade present income for future income only on more favorable terms than before.

But can we suppose that desires for present income can be

changed without changing desires for future income? Of course not. The factors which make one want future consumption or assets are much the same as those which make one want current consumption. If a man becomes less well satisfied with a given current consumption, must he not also be less well satisfied by the prospect of a given retirement income? Similarly if he saves for contingencies, the amount required to cover a period of unemployment is increased if his current consumption standard increases. The same considerations apply to attempts to leave inheritances. What appeared to be a generous provision for children at one period is inadequate at another because current consumption standards have increased.

With respect to "irrational" motives for saving, the problem is more difficult. If a man wishes to have assets merely for the sake of having assets, we cannot say that the amount he requires is increased by an increase in his current consumption. But it would be even more unreasonable to say that the psychological significance of assets runs in absolute terms. If a man had a thousand dollars in his mattress in 1850 he was a relatively rich man. A thousand-dollar hoard would be much less significant today. The standards of miserliness change with the general standard of living as much as anything else.

In the last section we argued that, with respect to current consumption, the utility index for any individual depends not on the absolute level of his consumption, but on the ratio of his expenditures to those of other people. We can now extend that proposition. Attitudes toward future consumption depend on current consumption standards. Current consumption standards or desires are influenced by other people's consumption behavior, and desires for future consumption will be influenced in the same way.

When interdependence of preferences is neglected, we make the original utility index depend on consumption and assets in the current period and at each date in the future. We write $U_i = F_i(C_{i1}, \ldots C_{in}, A_i, \ldots A_{in})$ where U_i is the utility index of the ith individual, C_{ik} is consumption expenditure of the ith individual in the kth time period, and A_{ik} is the value of his assets in the kth period.

We now take into account the influence of other people's consumption by dividing through each of the variables by $R_i = \Sigma \alpha_{ij} C_j$, that is, by a weighted average of the consumption expenditures of other individuals. α_{ij} is the weight applied to consumption of the jth individual by the ith individual. We now have $U_i = f_i(C_{i1}/R_i, \ldots C_{in}/R_i, A_{i1}/R_i \ldots A_{in}/R_i)$. The value of R_i is taken as a parameter by each individual. This is equivalent to measuring everything in units of other people's consumption expenditure. The maximization for a single individual is just the same as in the familiar case except for the character of the units. He can be supposed to choose his current consumption and plan his future in such a way as to maximize U_i subject to the restraints imposed by actual and expected incomes, interest rates, and assets. This will lead to a set of equations for each individual. With one kind of assets and one kind of consumption and a horizon of n periods, there will be $2n$ equations. (If there are several kinds of assets and several consumption goods, more equations will be introduced — expectations about each price and interest rate will also appear.) If there are r individuals in the system, there will be, altogether, $2rn$ equations. We are interested only in actual behavior at the current moment (not in planned behavior). By elimination we can solve for each individual's current consumption in terms of the variables which are objective to him, viz., current income, current assets, expected future (non-interest) income, expected future interest rates, current consumption of other people. We then have r equations of the form

$$C_i/R_i = f(Y_{i1}/R_i, \ldots Y_{in}/R_i, A_i/R_i \; r_1, r_2, \ldots, r_n)$$

where the Y_i's are expected incomes, the r's interest rates and A current assets. The equation takes the indicated form because we have the ordinary situation except for putting everything in units of other people's consumption. There are r unknown C_i's and r equations so that there is an equilibrium value for everyone's consumption. (The uniqueness and stability of the equilibrium are discussed below.)

We can now consider the character of the equilibrium. Our objective is to find how the equilibrium savings ratio varies with income. We are concerned with comparative statics not with dynamics. Consequently we will not try to follow through all the adjustments resulting from a change in income. Instead we shall compare the equilibrium position corresponding to one income with that corresponding to another. We compare the situation associated with per capita real income y_1 with that associated with per capita real income y_2. We assume that all other variables are the same in both cases, i.e., (1) income distribution (in the Lorenze curves sense) is the same so that every income is increased by a factor k, (2) interest rates and expected future interest rates are the same, (3) the relation between actual current incomes and expected future incomes is the same, (4) the last three assumptions imply that assets have increased by a factor k,[7] (5) population age distribution is constant.

Now what is the effect of the increase in income under these conditions? Since we have not specified the equations we cannot express our results in terms of the parameters. Nevertheless, the form of the equation permits us to discover the relation of the aggregate savings ratio to income under the specified conditions. Our equations are of the form

$$C_i/R_i = f(Y_{i1}/R_i, \ldots Y_{in}/R_i, A/R_i, r_1 \ldots r_n)$$

where $R_i = \Sigma \alpha_{ij} C_j$. Suppose a certain set of C_i's is a solution for given values of the y's, A's and r's. Suppose all the y's and A's are increased proportionately by a factor k. If all the C_i's rose by a factor k would the resulting set of C_i's be a solution? It can be seen at once that it would be. The ratios of $C_i/\Sigma \alpha_{ij} C_i$ would be unchanged if numerator and denominator were changed proportionately. Similarly the ratios $Y_{i1}/\Sigma \alpha_{ij} C_j$, etc. and $A_i/\Sigma \alpha_{ij} C_j$ would be unchanged. By assumption the interest rates are unchanged. If, therefore, the initial set of C_i's was a solution for the original income, the new set obtained by multiplying

---

[7] This is so because the value of assets is only the discounted value of future incomes from them. If the income distribution is the same we can assume that the division of income between property and other incomes is the same. Then actual and expected future property incomes have increased by a factor k. Since the interest rate is the same, the value of income-producing property increases in the same proportion.

each of the old C_i's by k is a solution when each income is multiplied by k. It follows that *in equilibrium, consumption is proportionate to income and the savings ratio is independent of the absolute level of income.*

We still have to deal with a number of problems. First, we have used a comparative statics analysis. Can such an analysis explain the observed phenomena in a dynamic world? That depends on the speed of change of the independent variable and the speed of adjustment. It is a fair description of actual movements of income to say that they are of two major types, (1) in prosperous periods income rises fairly steadily (with minor fluctuations) at a rate of 2–3 per cent per annum. (2) In depressions income first falls, then rises, both movements being rapid by comparison with those of the prosperous periods. When full employment is reached, income will be found to be higher than at the start of the depression. Chapter V is devoted to the analysis of cyclical movements in income, that is, to the analysis of the depression trough. The present argument is supposed to apply to periods of slow and fairly steady growth in income. When income grows in that manner, the speed of adjustment of consumption is high relative to the speed of movement of income. We can, therefore, safely use a comparative statics analysis without worrying about lagged adjustments.

7. STABILITY OF EQUILIBRIUM

Next we can ask what can be said about the character of the movement from one equilibrium position to another. This is necessary in order to see whether a change in the independent variable does in fact set up forces leading the dependent variable toward its new equilibrium. Suppose the system is in equilibrium at one level of income. Then let incomes increase by a few per cent while other conditions remain the same.

In general, we should expect people to split the increase between increased spending and increased saving. Moreover, we should expect saving (in the first adjustment) to increase as a percentage of income. We expect the savings ratio to increase with income (when the consumption of others is given) for familiar reasons. At (relatively) low incomes the desires for present consumption outweigh considerations of the future to such an extent that little or no saving occurs. At higher levels the pressure for increased current consumption is sufficiently reduced to permit some attention to the future. This increase in the relative importance of the future will continue until at some high level of income time preference is altogether overcome and consumption and saving advance in proportion. All this is familiar and need not be spelled out here. But all these arguments apply only when we consider changes in income of one consumer with the consumption of the others given.

Let us return to our consideration of a general change in income. The first adjustment involves an increase in consumption and an increase in saving for each individual. Saving increases more than in proportion to income. But that result was achieved when each consumer took his neighbors' consumption as a datum.

In fact, however, everyone increases his consumption. That means that for each individual $C_i/\Sigma\alpha_{ii}C_j$ has not increased as much as he thought when the denominator was fixed.[8] He is surrounded by superior goods to nearly the same extent as before. Their presence will induce him to give up some of his increased saving in favor of further increases in consumption. The same thing will happen to other people, and the whole process will be repeated. It will continue until the new equilibrium position, characterized by proportional increase in consumption, is reached.

By analogy we could put the argument another way. For each consumer the expression $1/\Sigma\alpha_{ij}C_j$ plays the role of a scale factor analogous to the price level. If a man gets an increase in money income he may plan to increase his savings ratio, but if he finds that the price level has increased in proportion to the increase in income he ends up in the position from which he started.

The argument just given indicates that there are forces which push the system in the direction of the equilibrium. We can conclude then that the equilibrium is a stable one. It can also be seen that at any point of time the savings ratio will be higher for those with (relatively) high incomes, which corresponds to the

---

[8] I do not mean to imply that anyone deliberately calculates the ratio of his expenditures to those of other people.

budget study results. But, as we have shown, that does not imply that the savings ratio will rise with increases in aggregate income. It is clear that when the Lorenze curve is given, the savings ratio depends on position in the income distribution rather than upon absolute income.

8. CONSTANCY OF THE SAVINGS RATIO

We can now turn to another problem. So far we have used a comparative statics analysis. Moreover, we have restricted ourselves to consideration of only one variable. We have held constant interest rates, and income expectation factors. Further we assumed that the time preference parameters were constant. If we want to test our analysis against the facts we have to give some consideration to the role of the other factors. A great deal has been written about the role of the interest rate and income expectations, but more heat than light has resulted. Until some new empirical evidence is introduced, it is doubtful whether further progress can be made in analysis of these factors. However, it is possible to side-step the problem. We can show that the long-term movements in the savings ratio are bound within fairly narrow limits regardless of changes in the factors under discussion.

It appears that about 75 per cent of spending units save virtually nothing.[9]

[9] It is very difficult to be exact about this point. The 1935–36 budget study is the only one which gives savings figures by city. But for our purposes it is not satisfactory to use the national totals. In the total figures the $3000–$3500 group, for example, would include families at about the 12th percentile (from the top) of the Chicago income distribution and at the 5th percentile in small cities of the midwest. For our purposes we need to consider the level of saving in relation to position in the local income distribution. In the 1935–36 study, saving fell below 5 per cent of income at about the 35th percentile in most cities. However, the study in question left out the relief population, most of whom would normally fall in the lower part of the distribution. The statement that about 75 per cent save less than 5 per cent is justified on that ground. About 50 per cent of families saved nothing, and considerable numbers had deficits. The 5 per cent saved by the families at the top of the group in question is probably an exaggeration if taken as an estimate of their average savings. Individual incomes fluctuate (even with a constant aggregate). A group in the upper part of the income distribution will contain a greater proportion of families whose income in the reporting period is above their average income than of families whose current income is below average. Their savings in the reporting year will therefore be higher than average.

Most of these families will not be influenced in their savings by changes in interest rates, income expectations, or even by changes in their own preference parameters. This is so because of a sharp discontinuity in preference functions. At (relatively) low levels of income, desires for current consumption are so strong that they overcome all considerations of the future. On the other hand the cost of dissaving (except temporarily) is too great to be borne. It is first of all difficult to achieve, secondarily, borrowing without repaying is usually considered to be unwise as well as immoral. Families in this range of incomes then have to balance their budgets on the average. Increases in desires for current consumption or decreases in the strength of motives for saving cannot affect them because of the high psychic costs of dissaving. Similarly changes in the interest rate or improvements in expectations of future income (except very spectacular ones) cannot reduce their saving, that is, make it more negative. On the other hand, changes which might lead them to save more will not have any effect unless they are large enough to overcome the unsatisfied current consumption desires. Because of the cost of dissaving, desires for current consumption and desires for future income have not been balanced at the margin. Small changes in interest rates, income expectations, or preference parameters cannot have any effect. Of course, some people will be just on the border line and will be affected. But the changes in question will not reach very far down into the zero saving group and will have only a small influence.

Theories which make consumption choices depend on the absolute level of income would not be inconsistent with the above argument. But those theories would lead one to expect that, as income rose, more and more people would get into a range of incomes beyond the discontinuity. Our theory shows why the people in lower parts of the income distribution are always below the discontinuity regardless of the absolute level of income.

It does not follow from this that changes in the factors under discussion will have no effect. For the upper quarter of the income distribution gets about half of the aggregate income. But if these factors produce a given change in the savings ratio of the upper group, the aggregate savings ratio will change by only half as much. If the upper quarter changes its average saving ratio from 10 per cent to 20 per cent, the aggregate ratio will change only from 5 per cent to 10 per cent. Moreover, a considerable part of this upper group saves only 10–15 per cent of its income. The income effects of changes in the interest rate will be rather small for them. Finally, we have to keep in mind that some of the factors which might change preference parameters have operated more strongly on the lower income groups than on the upper.

9. THE ROLE OF POPULATION GROWTH

One important aspect of the aggregation problem remains to be considered. A considerable part of all saving is done with a view to future liquidation. All those people who save in order to have assets to spend in retirement, or to provide for dependents in the event of death, plan to liquidate their savings in the future. We have little information on the relative importance of these motives for saving, but no one will deny that a very large part of saving is done either for retirement or protection of dependents. Saving for contingencies and future purchases of durable goods, or education of children, falls into the same class.[10]

To the extent that saving for retirement is important, the age distribution of the population and the rate of growth of income will be important in the determination of the rate of saving. These variables are important because they determine the size

[10] "When asked their purpose in saving, about three out of five spending units mentioned motives which can be classified under the general heading of 'security.' Old age, ill health, unemployment and general protection against a 'rainy day' come under this head. Old age and ill health together were specifically mentioned far more frequently than unemployment, perhaps indicating that people expect little unemployment or that they no longer consider protection against unemployment an individual responsibility. A further one out of five save to make investments (mainly to purchase a home, but including some business investment as well), and one out of six to provide benefits for children (mainly education). Only one out of ten indicated that they were saving to purchase consumer durable goods or to make other consumption expenditures, while one in twelve mentioned miscellaneous reasons, or had no specific purpose." "A National Survey of Liquid Assets," *Federal Reserve Bulletin* (July 1946), p. 720.

of negative saving by retired persons relative to the size of positive savings by persons preparing for retirement.

Indeed if all saving was done for retirement, a community with stable population and income would have zero aggregate saving. Once the age distribution had reached equilibrium, the dissavings of retired persons would just balance off the positive savings of young people. A growing society with stable income per capita will have positive savings even if every individual liquidates all his savings before he dies. By comparison with a stable population, a growing one will have a larger proportion of young people and a smaller proportion of old people. The savings of the young people will more than balance off the dissavings of the older ones. The aggregate savings ratio will therefore vary with the age distribution of the population even with constant income per capita.

Even a stable population would have positive net savings if it had a rising income per capita. But the connection between the rate of increase of income and the rate of saving is not a simple one. First, suppose that the value of assets is simply the accumulated amount of past savings. This would be the case if savers simply put their money in banks and the government borrowed it at zero interest to make wars. If in these circumstances income increased without affecting asset values, the rate of saving would be directly connected with the rate of growth of income. Suppose each age group saved (positively or negatively) a constant fraction of its income. Then, with constant population and income, dissavings and savings would just balance off. But with rising income they would not. For the bank accounts of the dissavers would depend on a weighted average of past incomes. If people saved during ages 20 to 60 and dissaved during ages 60 to 80 the amount of dissavings made by the retired people in year t would depend on the size of incomes during years $t-60$ to $t-1$. The positive savings of those still earning would depend on current income, which by assumption, is higher than the past income. If each individual planned to die with zero assets the positive savings would have to be greater than the negative ones.

This model, however, is certainly unrealistic. Assets are not equal to the sum of past savings. As was pointed out above, asset values are essentially equal to the present value of expected future incomes from property (that proposition is seriously modified by the presence of a large volume of government securities).

Increases in per capita income occur largely as the result of the adoption of new techniques of production. These new techniques may or may not involve net capital expenditure but in any case the assets created by the process are not directly dependent on the amount of savings invested. The savings will have to be invested somewhere but one cannot judge the increase in assets by the rate of savings. The amount of assets available for liquidation by old people will thus depend on the extent to which they share in the results of the innovation process. If, for example, old people hold a cross section of all types of assets, the amounts they have for liquidation will increase in proportion to income. In this case their dissaving ought to rise as fast as the positive saving of young people. Consequently a stable population with rising income could have no net saving (if all saving were for retirement purposes).

If on the other hand the retired population buys annuities or fixed interest securities they will not share in the capital gains associated with increases in income. The rate of saving will then be dependent on the rate of increase of income.

Actually some old people will hold fixed income securities while others hold common stocks or retain interests in businesses. This would not make any difference if there were no relation between the type of assets held and the dissaving plans of the individuals concerned. It is probable, however, that the people who save to retire by liquidating assets will be middle class types who will hold safe fixed income securities. On the other hand people in the higher brackets may be able to live off the income from business interests and pass control of a firm to their heirs. Thus those who dissave in retirement will be those who gain least by innovations. The rate of increase of income will thus be one of the important determinants of the rate of net saving.

10. The Distribution of Income

In recent years there have been a good many discussions about the possibility of changing the aggregate propensity to save by redistributing income. In these discussions it has been assumed that the effect of a redistribution can be judged by changing the weights applied to budget study data. That procedure is legitimate only on the assumption that individual consumption preferences are independent. If that is not so a decrease in inequality might *increase* the average propensity to save.

There are no data which permit us to estimate the effect of any given redistribution. However, a simple example will suffice to show the general character of the movements which might result.

Let us suppose that a ceiling is placed on incomes at (say) $5000 at 1941 prices. All income in excess of $5000 is taken in taxes and given to the lower income groups. Suppose, for the sake of the argument, that all other conditions including the growth rate of income remain unchanged. Eventually then every family would have an income of $5000. How would saving be affected? Initially, of course, the savings ratio would fall. Those who lost income would dissave while those who gained would spend the whole increase. But consider the situation after a period sufficiently long to permit full adaptation to the new situation.

Those who had $5000 can be expected to save at least as much as before. The reduction in expenditure by the former high income receivers increases the value of $C_i/\Sigma \alpha_{ij} C_j$ for the $5000 group. Consequently the latter group should behave like people with an increase in relative income. This would lead them to save, if anything, more than before. For simplicity suppose they save only the same amount. In 1941 the $5000 income group saved about 25 per cent of income.

As the incomes of the others advance they will gradually move into the $5000 group and remain there. They can be expected to save as much as those who had $5000 in the first place. The aggregate savings ratio would approach 25 per cent then. That figure is to be compared with the one which would have resulted had the distribution remained unchanged. The aggregate savings ratio in the past has seldom been above 10 per cent. Our theory indicates that a rise in income will not in itself tend to raise the ratio. We must conclude then that the savings ratio *may* be increased by equalization measures.

Of course, the example just given is extremely unrealistic; but it at least shows that there is considerable doubt as to how saving would be affected by a redistribution.

11. CONCLUSIONS

Our results can be summarized as follows:

(1) The aggregate savings ratio is independent of the absolute level of aggregate income.

(2) The aggregate savings ratio is dependent on (a) interest rates, (b) the relation between current and expected future incomes, (c) the distribution of income, (d) the age distribution of the population, (e) the rate of growth of income.

(3) Because of the discontinuity in preference functions the aggregate savings ratio will be rather insensitive to changes in interest rates, expectations, and preference parameters. Large changes in these factors will be required to produce substantial changes in the savings ratio.

(4) Cet. par. the propensity to save of an individual can be regarded as a rising function of his percentile position in the income distribution. The parameters of that function will change with changes in the shape of the income distribution.

Partly for expositional reasons we have put our argument in a somewhat more blunt and unqualified way than is justified. What we have done is to present a hypothesis about consumer behavior and work out some of its implications. In the nature of the case we have had to oversimplify. Much of the richness and variety of real life must be lost in developing a hypothesis which can be stated formally. Moreover, we have not proved our hypothesis. Indeed we cannot. All we can do is set up a theory which seems plausible in the light of general observation and of psychological considerations. Having done that, we can see whether the implications of the hypothesis are consistent with available data. If they are, we can tentatively accept the hypothesis. But we have to recognize that new data may break it down at any time.

CHAPTER IV

A THEORY VERSUS THE FACTS

Now THAT we have a hypothesis we must see how it works. No amount of data can prove a hypothesis, but they can disprove it. All we can do is to take the available materials and see whether they are consistent with our theory. If they are, then we are in a position to say that our hypothesis is at least as good as any other hypothesis which also fits the data. We can then look at other hypotheses and see how they fit the data. If it can be shown that existing alternative hypotheses are inconsistent with observation, then we are left with a single theory which must, for the moment, be accepted. That does not mean that it is true. It merely means that it is the only acceptable working hypothesis. New data which destroy it may appear tomorrow and with them new theories will appear.

Unfortunately we cannot even make clear-cut tests of existing hypotheses. Data on long-run movements of saving and income are scarce and inaccurate. Data on the other elements in the problem are almost nonexistent. Consequently we can only set forth such facts as are known and make judgments as to the plausibility of one hypothesis or another. In the circumstances we cannot use single pieces of data to make critical tests. We shall have to consider a wide range of data and try to establish our position by the weight of evidence. Even then I fear that we shall only get off with a Scotch verdict.

We shall begin with some direct tests of our own hypothesis. One of these tests is based on an interview study of income aspirations. A second involves a comparison of Negro and white saving. A third is based on comparisons of savings in different cities and income groups. Next we turn to the problem of changes in saving over time. We show that our hypothesis is consistent with such facts as are known in this field. The alternative, that the propensity to consume is dependent on absolute income and trend factors is shown to be at least implausible.

1. INCOME ASPIRATION AND SOCIAL STATUS

We have argued that a consumer's utility index varies with the ratio of his consumption to a weighted average of other people's consumption. Moreover, we tried to show that the weights depend on the relationship between the individuals in question. Any particular consumer will be more influenced by the consumption of people with whom he has social contacts than by that of people with whom he has only casual contacts.

Consider two groups with the same incomes. One group associates with people who have the same income as they have. The other group associates with people who have higher incomes than the members of the group. The expression $\Sigma a_{ij} C_j$ will have a greater value for the second group than for the first. The two groups have the same income but the first will be better satisfied with its position than the second. Its members will make fewer unfavorable comparisons between their consumption standard and that of their associates.

A study of income aspirations made for a different purpose makes it possible for us to test the hypothesis just set forth.

In a study made by the Office of Public Opinion Research[1] a sample of persons supposed to be representative were asked to give their weekly income and to answer the following question. "About how much more money than that (i.e. the stated weekly income) do you think your family would need to have the things that might make your family happier or more comfortable than it is now?" Since a large number reported themselves satisfied with their present income the results were also tabulated on the criterion of satisfaction or dissatisfaction. The results are summarized in Table 1.

It will be noted that the percentage increase wanted falls steadily as income increases until the highest group is reached. This phenomenon is explained by the authors of the study by

[1] R. Centers and H. Cantril, "Income Satisfaction and Income Aspiration," *Journal of Abnormal and Social Psychology* (January 1946).

the fact that the dissatisfied members of the over $100 group have a higher social status than is indicated by their incomes.

TABLE 1

INCOME AND INCOME ASPIRATION*

Weekly Income	Cases	Dis-satisfied	Satis-fied	No Opinion	No. Specify-ing Amount More Wanted	In-creased Income Wanted in Per-centage	Income Wanted in Dollars
		%	%	%		%	
National	1,165	56	32	12	581	86	$ ...
Under $20	163	68	16	16	100	162	16.20
$20–29.99	170	72	19	9	116	97	24.25
$30–39.99	207	67	20	13	129	66	23.10
$40–59.99	310	54	35	11	147	59	29.50
$60–99.99	191	43	49	8	73	52	41.60
Over $100	124	20	66	14	16	100	100.00

* "Income Satisfaction and Income Aspiration," *Journal of Abnormal and Social Psychology*, Vol. 41, No. 1.

A closer examination of the cases in this category reveals, however, that this large increase is due to the presence in this group of a considerable proportion of professional people and that it is they who want the relatively large increases. Our data do not provide any direct evidence as to why this is so but they suggest that it is because at this level, physicians, lawyers and college professors are competing for social status with persons far above them in income, so that the relatively large increases desired represent a wish to strengthen an already high social status with a relatively high income status. In a previous study on the social and economic class identifications of various occupational groups by Wallace, Williams and Cantril it was found that there existed a large discrepancy between the two identifications for professional people. In their study, while 11% of professional people identified themselves as upper class socially only 5% so classed themselves economically. Another pertinent finding is that of Smith who reports that inferiority feelings are more prevalent among the children of professional people than among those of any other group.[2]

[2] *Ibid.*

The results of the Princeton study as well as the interpretation given by the authors of the study are exactly those predicted by our hypothesis.

2. NEGRO AND WHITE SAVINGS

The differences between consumption expenditures of Negroes and whites at the same income level should also provide a test for the validity of our hypothesis. Since the Negroes of large cities generally live in neighborhoods separate from those in which whites live, and do not compete for social status with whites or have any very close social contacts with them, we have in effect two separate communities. At the same time these two communities are subjected to the same ways of doing things. Moreover, the ranking of goods is about the same in the two communities. If impulses to consume arise principally out of the fact that goods fulfill some sort of objective need, then Negroes might be expected to save about the same amount at a given level of income as whites. But if the theory set out in the last chapter is correct then Negroes should save more at every level of money income (since the group as a whole is poorer). We should in fact expect that Negroes in a given percentile position in the Negro income distribution would save as much as whites in the same percentile position. The data of the Consumer Purchases Study of 1935–36 bear out this prediction. A comparison of the savings of Negroes and whites in New York and Columbus made by Mendershausen[3] yields the following result:

City	Break Even Point	Standardized Savings Per Cent	Average Income
New York			
Whites..................	$2290	−2.2	$ ...
Negroes................	1530	6.7	1379
Columbus			
Whites..................	1310	7.9	2080
Negroes................	910	20.8	1141

[3] Horst Mendershausen, "Differences in Family Savings Between Cities of Different Sizes and Locations, Whites and Negroes," *Review of Economic Statistics* (August 1940).

The Standardized Savings per cent is obtained by weighting savings and income for each money income level by the proportion of national population receiving that income in 1935–36.

CHART I—SAVING PERCENTAGES VS. POSITION IN INCOME DISTRIBUTION 1935–36

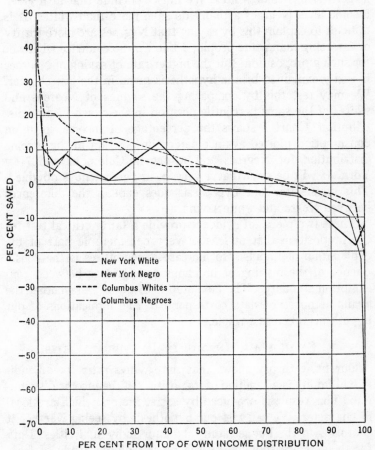

The results are thus independent of the local income distribution. Both New York and Columbus Negroes saved about three times as much on the average as whites at the corresponding income levels. It can, of course, be argued that at lower levels of income Negroes run smaller deficits because they cannot obtain credit or because the temporarily unemployed form a smaller proportion of the low-income group among Negroes than among whites. But these factors cannot be used to explain the fact that at higher levels of income Negroes have much larger savings than whites. We must conclude that at a given income level Negroes actually do save more than whites. It is difficult to explain this by saying that Negroes are more thrifty or farseeing than white people; I know of no evidence whatever for such a proposition. But the higher rate of saving of Negroes is easily explained by the hypothesis given in the last chapter. We may test this by comparing the savings of Negroes and whites at the same percentile position in their own income distribution. Chart I shows the percentage of income spent on consumption plotted against percentile position in the income distribution for Negroes and whites in Columbus and New York. It will be seen that a very good agreement is obtained. This means that our hypothesis does explain the differences between Negro and white saving.

These two pieces of evidence provide a fairly critical test for the proposition that at least a very considerable part of the explanation of impulses to increase expenditures is the consequence of the making of invidious comparisons between consumption standards. The next step is to try to see whether the available observed data correspond to the implications of our hypothesis taken as a whole.

3. SAVINGS AND INCOME IN INDIVIDUAL CITIES

Our basic theory shows that the savings ratio for an individual family is a function of its position in the income distribution. This result is produced by social factors which are local in character. We can test our hypothesis by seeing whether it conforms to the budget study data for individual cities. Data for the test are supplied by the reports of the Study of Consumer Purchases made in 1935–36.[4] In making the test we have left out the lower part of the distribution because families in

[4] U. S. Bureau of Labor Statistics, *Bulletins* 642–649.

that range reported serious unemployment. No income classes have been included for which an average of less than forty-eight full weeks of employment was reported. This was done on the ground that the unemployed are likely to spend an especially high proportion of their income, for they try, to some extent, to maintain the living standard they had when fully employed.[5] This point is discussed in detail in the chapter on short-run variations in saving.

It should be noted that the income distributions as given in the Consumer Purchase Study reports are incomplete. The distributions are restricted to Native White unbroken families who were not on relief at any time during the reporting year. The families left out would for the most part have appeared at the bottom of the income distribution. This means that if (say) 20 per cent of the families were left out, the percentile position of a family in the reported distribution would differ from its percentile position in the total distribution by a multiplier factor of 1.2. Since we propose to relate the percentage of income saved to the logarithm of the percentile position, this results in the addition of a constant factor to the independent variable and will not, therefore, affect our results seriously.

The relation $y = a \log X + b$ (where y is percentage of income spent on consumption and X is percentile position in the local income distribution) was fitted to the data for a number of cities. The results are shown in Table 2.

The figures in the column headed y_{100} indicate the expected expenditure of families at the 100th percentile from the top of the income distribution, that is, the very poorest families. It will be noted that no data on families near this range were included in the calculation, for the expenditure patterns of very low-income families shown in the Consumer Purchases Study data were seriously affected by unemployment. In a period of full employment, however, we would expect the poorest families in any community to spend all of their income and perhaps run slight deficits. The fact that our regressions when pro-

[5] Elizabeth W. Gilboy, *Applicants for Work Relief* (Cambridge: Harvard University Press, 1940).

jected to the 100th percentile show expected expenditures of just over 100 per cent is, therefore, a confirmation of the reasonableness of the regressions. In view of the fact that the correlations are uniformly high and the regression coefficients of the same order of magnitude, it seems clear that the data are entirely consistent with our hypothesis.

TABLE 2

RELATIONS BETWEEN THE SAVINGS RATIO AND POSITION IN THE INCOME DISTRIBUTION

City	a	σa	b	σb	$\bar{y}$	σy	y_{100}	σy_{100}	r_{xy}
Columbus........	18.06	1.88	65.15	2.06	82.67	1.03	101.27	2.25	.972
Providence.......	15.06	2.21	74.98	2.31	89.62	.85	105.10	2.43	.948
Denver..........	14.12	2.30	72.35	2.55	86.71	1.03	100.59	2.48	.936
Chicago..........	12.96	.97	75.43	1.08	87.81	.55	101.35	1.16	.989
Omaha...........	8.85	1.67	78.54	1.75	86.54	.90	96.24	2.03	.909
Middle Size									
West Central.....	19.21	4.64	76.92	5.14	85.94	2.5	95.34	5.34	.951
Middle Size									
Rocky Mts.......	16.01	2.78	74.38	3.20	91.17	1.3	106.40	2.95	.909
Middle Size									
East Central......	20.20	2.92	63.91	3.37	85.56	1.3	104.31	2.99	.933
Small East									
Central..........	19.17	3.36	65.60	4.75	92.00	1.03	103.94	2.11	.932
Small North									
Central..........	23.52	.89	52.97	1.17	86.91	.30	100.01	.71	.997
Small Plains									
and Mts..........	17.76	3.47	67.66	4.94	92.32	1.07	103.18	2.12	.918
11 Cities........	15.21	.82	71.54	.93	87.77	.19	101.98	.92	.897

However, the results shown above do not provide a critical test of our hypotheses as against the view that the percentage of income spent is a function of absolute money or real income. For, when the percentage of income spent is fitted to money income it is found that just as good results are obtained. Money income and percentile position are related by a linear logarithmic relation. Consequently we cannot disprove either hypothesis by means of this test. We can only say that our hypothesis is not inconsistent with the observations.

4. LONG PERIOD VARIATIONS IN SAVING

Our hypothesis has stood up well enough so far. Now we have to face the difficult task of evaluating its consistency with variations in aggregate savings over time. This task is difficult for two reasons. First the data on savings are limited and not very accurate. Second our hypothesis leads to a definite prediction only when certain factors are held constant. Before we can test it we shall have to make some judgments about variations in the non-income factors entering our hypothesis.

The only data on long period variations in aggregate savings are those given by Kuznets.

Kuznets has given data on Capital Formation and National Income by decades for the period 1879–1938. The figures are shown in Table 3;[8] they include corporate as well as individual saving.

TABLE 3

CAPITAL FORMATION AND NATIONAL INCOME BY DECADES, 1879–1938

Decade	1	2	3	4	5	6
	Current Prices			1929 Prices		
	Net Nat'l Prod.	Net Cap. Form.	1 as % of 2	Net Nat'l Prod.	Net Cap. Form.	4 as % of 5
1879–1888.......	10,310	1073	10.4	15,175	1766	11.6
1884–1893.......	11,527	1348	11.7	18,087	2524	14.0
1889–1898.......	12,425	1489	12.0	21,189	3145	14.8
1894–1903.......	15,084	1747	11.6	26,126	3509	13.4
1899–1908.......	20,615	2329	11.3	32,402	4110	12.7
1904–1913.......	26,640	2918	11.0	38,744	4808	12.4
1909–1918.......	36,934	4158	11.3	45,034	5817	12.9
1914–1923.......	55,949	6489	11.6	53,826	6250	11.6
1919–1928.......	71,887	7792	10.8	68,598	6905	10.1
1924–1933.......	70,064	4652	6.6	73,316	4247	5.8
1929–1938.......	61,274	1930	3.1	71,110	1610	2.3

[8] Simon Kuznets, *Uses of National Income in Peace and War*, Occasional Paper No. 6 (New York: National Bureau of Economic Research, 1942). (Figures are in millions of dollars.)

For our purposes the series in current prices is the relevant one. We are concerned with variations in the proportion of income that consumers are willing to save. The percentages saved calculated in 1929 prices differ from those in current prices only because the prices of capital goods did not change in proportion to the prices of consumers' goods. But we are not interested in what investors got for their money but only in what level of income was required to get consumers (and corporations) to save as much in money terms as was invested. If consumer saving is a function of real consumer income then the price of capital goods is irrelevant to the savers.

The savings in the last two decades were abnormally low, because of the depression of the thirties. Since this period is discussed in detail in Chapter V we shall consider here only the data for the decades up to 1929.

The Kuznets data do not show any trend in the savings ratio. Unfortunately the data are not entirely reliable. To judge from the recently issued Commerce Department data Kuznets appears to have overestimated consumers' savings in the period 1929–1938. Whether the same bias holds throughout these data it is impossible to tell. Nevertheless his data allow us to make a judgment about the movement of the savings ratio. We have to allow for some upward bias in the Kuznets data. We also have to reduce his figures to allow for corporate saving. On the other hand his data are on a national product rather than a disposable income basis. But in the period in question personal taxes and transfer payments were rather small. Allowing for these corrections it would seem safe to say that personal savings in the decades from 1870 to 1929 have varied between (say) 5 per cent and 10 per cent of income. Our general information on capital formation in that period will certainly support the conclusion that saving in that period must have been at least 5 per cent of income in every decade.

There cannot have been much of a trend in the savings ratio. Personal savings in 1929 were 4.5 per cent of disposable income. On the same conceptual basis the Kuznets data indicate that personal savings in the earlier years of the twenties ranged from 5 per cent to 7 per cent of disposable income. There is, therefore, no evidence of any appreciable trend in the savings ratio.

According to our hypothesis, the savings ratio is independent of the absolute level of income. It may vary, however, with any of a number of other factors. Before we compare our theory with the data we shall have to discuss the role of those factors. The factors in question are (1) the interest rate, (2) the relation between current and expected incomes, (3) the distribution of income, (4) the age distribution of the population, (5) the rate of growth of income, (6) changes in attitudes toward saving. Two other factors discussed by supporters of the view that the savings ratio does depend on the absolute level of income are (7) the trend toward urbanization, and (8) the introduction of new products.

We can now try to compare our theory with the leading alternative theory. According to our theory the savings ratio is independent of the absolute level of income. If, over a long period of rising income, the net influence of the factors just listed is small we can predict an approximately constant savings ratio. On the other hand, if those factors operate in such a way as to discourage saving we should predict a falling ratio. The savings ratio was in fact approximately constant. Therefore our theory can be disproved by showing that trend factors tending to discourage saving were in operation.

The situation is just the opposite in regard to the other theory. The Keynesian consumption function as used by such writers as Smithies[7] consists of two parts.

(1) A linear relationship between real disposable income per capita and real consumer expenditure per capita. The constant term is positive and the slope is less than one. Consequently as income rises consumer expenditures fall as a percentage of income.

(2) A trend factor which produces an upward movement in the constant. The trend term offsets the tendency for the savings ratio to rise with income. The trend is supposed to be produced by introduction of new products or by urbanization. It explains why the savings ratio has been more or less steady

[7] "Forecasting Postwar Demand I," *Econometrica* (January 1945).

in the past. But the explanation is just the opposite to ours. We maintain that the savings ratio will be constant when trend factors are absent. The supporters of the view just described maintain that the savings ratio will rise unless it is offset by trend factors.

It is easy to see that both hypotheses can be tested at once. If the trend factors are shown to be powerful our hypothesis cannot explain the data. If they are shown to be weak our hypothesis can explain the data and the other cannot.

5. New Consumers' Products

To evaluate the influence of the introduction of new products is a difficult task. It really involves asking what would have happened had the new products not been invented. Nevertheless something can be said about the question. First we can distinguish two types of new products; those which make possible a new range of activities and those which represent improved ways of doing old things. The latter group can be subdivided into cases in which the improvement involves increased expense and those in which it involves decreased expense.

The same new product may, of course, play a dual role. It may make new activities possible and it may improve the way in which old things are done. Improvements in transportation for example have made possible a wider range of vacation activities. On the other hand they have made transportation in general more comfortable and convenient.

Many of the new household appliances fall into the cost-reducing category. They are essentially substitutes for maids. Had income increased as it has but without the invention of vacuum cleaners and washing machines, the demand for servants would have increased. Their wages would presumably have gone up even more than they have done. However that may be, it seems difficult to maintain that household appliances caused an increase in expenditure which would not otherwise have taken place.

These remarks at least show that the influence of new goods is not all in one direction. But is there any way to test the importance of new consumers' goods? In discussing this factor Kuznets[8] says,

Even a hasty glance at the make-up of consumers' outlay in recent decades will indicate how large a portion of it is commodities and services that are distinctly results of modern technology and relatively recent technical innovations. Among the perishables are certain drugs and toilet preparations and gasoline; among the semidurable, tires and tubes and certain types of house furnishings; among consumers durable, electrical household appliances and supplies, radios, passenger cars, etc.; among services not embodied in commodities services of professional practitioners vastly superior to those in the past, repair services in connection with the new types of consumers durable goods and the like.

The data on which Kuznets based his statement are those given by Shaw.[9] These figures show that the proportion of output devoted to the lines mentioned above has increased sharply over the last fifty years while the proportion going into other lines, particularly food, has decreased. The proportion of output of commodities going into Perishable items fell from 57.52 per cent in 1879–1889 to 50.04 per cent in 1929–1939. This movement included a drop from 47.76 per cent to 37.49 per cent for food and kindred products while Drug, Toilet, and Household preparations rose from 1.43 per cent to 2.68 per cent and Fuel and Lighting Products from 2.72 per cent to 4.34 per cent. Meanwhile, Consumers' Durables rose from 9.43 per cent to 16.39 per cent. The principal elements in the increase were the rise of Electrical Household Appliances, Radios, Motor Vehicles, and Motor Vehicles Accessories from zero to .73 per cent, .80 per cent, 6.18 per cent, and 1.41 per cent, respectively, while horse-drawn vehicles fell from 1.05 per cent to zero. The consumers' semi-durable group as a whole fell in importance from 23.01 per cent to 19.14 per cent. Within the group Dry Goods and Notions fell from 6.39 per cent to 2.20

[8] Kuznets, *Uses of National Income in Peace and War.*
[9] W. H. Shaw, *Finished Commodities Since 1879,* Occasional Paper No. 3 (New York: National Bureau of Economic Research, 1941).

per cent and Shoes from 4.81 per cent to 2.67 per cent, while Tires and Tubes rose from zero to 1.02 per cent. All other movements were comparatively minor. It can easily be seen that the principal element in shift of output is the automobile. Undoubtedly there were new product developments in other fields but short of tabulating Sears Roebuck catalogues it would be difficult to find them. In any case it seems apparent that the major developments in new goods were in the field of consumer durables. But the rate of introduction of new durables was not even throughout the period nor was it proportional to the growth rate of income per capita or per consuming unit. We may make use of this fact to test the efficacy of durables as a factor which offsets the tendency for saving to rise with rising income.

If it is the case that the proportion of income saved tends to rise with income but is offset by introduction of new durables, then during periods when this is taking place the proportion of income spent on durables should rise. Table 4 shows data for income per consuming unit, proportion of income saved, and proportion of consumers' outlay spent on durables.

TABLE 4*

INCOME PER CONSUMING UNIT, PROPORTION SAVED, AND
PROPORTION SPENT ON DURABLES, 1879–1928

Decade	Income per Consuming Unit	Per Cent Saved	Per Cent Spent Durables
1879–1888...................	406	10.4	6.2
1884–1893...................	428	11.7	6.7
1889–1898...................	450	12.0	6.5
1894–1903...................	502	11.6	6.2
1899–1908...................	562	11.3	6.1
1904–1913...................	610	11.0	6.5
1909–1918...................	652	11.3	7.9
1914–1923...................	723	11.6	9.9
1919–1928...................	851	10.8	12.0

* Based on Kuznets, *Uses of National Income in Peace and War.*

A study of the table indicates that up to the decade 1909–1918 the percentage of consumers' outlay spent on durables remained virtually constant. During this period real income per consuming unit increased by 50 per cent while the percentage of income saved remained practically constant. Thus, unless some set of important new goods in the non-durable classes can be shown to have influenced saving before 1909 we must conclude that the introduction of new goods does not provide an explanation of the stability of the percentage of income saved in the period before 1909. New durable goods did become important after 1909 but if savings were constant in the face of rising income before that date, they presumably would have continued to be so afterward even if new goods had not been introduced. If the automobile had not been invented people would have bought pianos and large houses, as they did before when they received higher incomes.

We may conclude then that there is not much *evidence* in favor of the proposition that new products have caused a strong upward trend in consumption.

6. URBANIZATION

It is well known that farm families have a higher propensity to save than city families. It can therefore be argued that a decrease in the relative size of the farm population causes a decrease in the aggregate propensity to save. Such a shift in population distribution has been going on for a long time. This fact has, therefore, been used as an explanation of the upward trend in consumption.

We may first note that the urbanization argument cannot be a complete explanation. For there has been an upward shift in the propensity to consume of *urban* families.[10]

Nevertheless the urbanization argument is correct, in the sense that urbanization must tend to produce some decrease in the aggregate savings ratio. The question is, how much of a change? The fact is that though the average and marginal propensity to save for farmers is higher at each income, their

[10] Louis Bean, "Relation of Disposable Income and the Business Cycle to Consumer Expenditure," *Review of Economic Statistics* (November 1946).

overall savings ratio is about the same as that for city families. This is so because farmers usually have relatively low incomes. Average farm savings now appear to bear about the same proportion to farm income as city savings to city income. The Study of Consumer Purchases indicates that in 1935–36 non-relief farm families saved 12.5 per cent of their aggregate incomes while urban non-relief families saved 10.7 per cent of income and rural non-farm families saved 12.3 per cent of income.[11] These figures are not of course strictly accurate nor are they directly applicable to long-period problems since they represent a year of depression. Agricultural income in 1935–36, however, formed about the same proportion of national income as it had for some years past. The period was not therefore particularly one of relative depression in agriculture. But since it is believed that the *marginal* propensity to save of farmers is higher than for city families, an upward movement of income would raise the percentage of income saved by farmers more than for city families. If, therefore, we suppose that in a year of about average employment farm savings (as a percentage of income) would bear a ratio of 3 to 2 to city savings, we should not be far wrong. Since average savings through the last two decades were about 10 per cent of income except in the worst years, and since farm income was about 10 per cent of total income, we may use 9.5 per cent for city savings and 14.2 per cent for farm savings. Weighted by a factor of 9 for city families and a factor of 1 for farm families, this will give average savings of 10 per cent. But fifty years ago farm income was about one-third of national income. Therefore, if the trend in income had continued and the other trends tending to reduce savings had also continued, the current average percentage saved would be $(14.2 + 2 \times 9.5)/3 = 11$ per cent. Thus the weighting factor cannot have accounted for more than a 1 per cent change in saving or about a 10 per cent reduction below the amount which would otherwise have been saved. Most of the offsets to the tendency for saving to rise with income must, therefore, have come from other factors.

[11] National Resources Committee, *Family Expenditures in the United States,* pp. 123, 127, 130.

7. THE AGE DISTRIBUTION OF THE POPULATION

We have already shown how the age distribution can affect the savings ratio. We must now consider what changes in age distribution have actually occurred. A number of elements are involved here. First, children under 15 form a decreasing proportion of the population. Thus, in 1910 32.1 per cent of the population were under 15. In 1940 only 25.1 per cent were under 15. Since children under 15 are in general not earners, a reduction in their numbers tends to make greater saving a possibility. On the other hand the proportion of persons in the retirement age group is increasing. In 1910 6.7 per cent of the population were over 60, while in 1940 this percentage had risen to 10.4 per cent.[12] Since retired persons either spend previously accumulated assets or live on their relatives, an increasing proportion of old people tends to reduce aggregate savings. If the two groups are aggregated, then the two classes formed 38.8 per cent of the population in 1910 and 35.5 per cent in 1940. It would be a mistake, however, to weight the two groups equally. No data are available on the dissavings of retired persons but it seems probable that an increase in the number of retired persons causes a greater reduction in savings than an equal increase in the number of children. If this is the case, then a reweighting of the two groups would result in almost complete cancellation of the effects of decreasing the number of children and increasing the number of old persons. It seems, therefore, that the net effect of these two aspects of population change is negligible.

There is, however, another aspect to change in the age distribution. Persons who are in the age groups just before sixty save substantially more than those in younger groups.[13] Thus a general increase in the age of the population within the group of working age will lead to an increase in saving. In 1910, 17.2 per cent of the population between 15 and 60 were in the age

---

[12] *Statistical Abstract of the United States* (1942), p. 23.

[13] "Family Spending and Saving as Related to Age of Wife and Number of Children, "U. S. Department of Agriculture, *Misc. Pub.* 489 (Washington, D. C., 1942).

group 40–49, while 11.7 per cent were in the age 50–59 group. By 1940 these percentages had increased to 20.0 and 15.3[14]

Thus the net effect of the change in the age distribution of the population seems to be to increase the propensity to save rather than to decrease it.

This factor tends to offset the decrease in savings resulting from the relative decrease in farm population and the urbanization of attitudes of the remaining farmers.

8. INCOME DISTRIBUTION

Very little can be said about changes in income distribution because very little is known about them. We do know that the proportion of income going to wages and salaries has remained nearly constant since 1870. High income taxes did not become a factor until very recently. Inequality among those reporting income for tax purposes did not show any marked trend during the twenties and thirties, though it did show some cyclical movement.[15] We must conclude that there is no evidence of a trend in the income distribution while there is some, albeit sketchy, evidence that inequality has been more or less constant.

9. THE RATE OF GROWTH OF INCOME

The effect of changes in the rate of growth of income depends on the way in which retired people hold their assets. If retired people who live by liquidating assets hold fixed income securities they will not share in increases in income. On the other hand if they hold equities they will share in the gains, at least partially, through capital gains (the extent to which they share increases will depend on the extent to which increases in income involve the flotation of new issues). For simplicity we shall assume that retired people hold only fixed income securities. We shall assume that in each year the assets of the group retiring bear a constant ratio to per capita income in that year. At retirement people switch into fixed income securities and

[14] *Statistical Abstract* (1942), p. 23.
[15] N. O. Johnson, "The Pareto Law," *Review of Economic Statistics* (February 1937).

liquidate them over the remainder of their lives. If income per capita is rising, current savings by young people will be based on current incomes. The assets available for liquidation, hence the rate of dissaving by retired people, will depend on past incomes. On our assumptions the net rate of saving will depend on the percentage increase in per capita income from one decade to the next. If the rate of increase is steady the savings ratio will be steady. If the rate of increase increases, net savings will rise, and vice versa. The income figure should be money income since the retired people's assets are fixed in money terms. The Kuznets figures in Table 4 show that *real* income per capita rose at 10 per cent per decade in the period 1877–1900, thereafter the increases were considerably greater though unsteady. Since prices were falling in the first period and rising thereafter, this effect is magnified. The changes in the growth rate of income then tended to increase saving from the early part of the period to the later part. The magnitude of the effect is probably not great but it tends to offset some of the factors which may have tended to reduce saving.

10. Interest Rates and Expectations

Expectations about future income enter the picture in two ways. Expectations about future personal service income enter the determination of savings plans. These plans are also affected by expectations about the future value of assets.

With respect to expectations about wages and salary income not much can be said. Various psychological factors enter into estimates of one's future earnings but no objective measure of these is available. To the extent that such expectations are based on experience, the growth of total income can be used as an index of expectations. We have shown that the income growth rate shows little trend so that we have no reason to expect a trend in the savings ratio on this account.

With respect to asset expectations the situation is different. There are objective indicators of the relation between current incomes and expected future incomes. When income increases the savings ratio will tend to increase if the value of assets rises less than proportionately and vice versa. The ratio of corporate income to asset values is indicated by the earnings ratios of common stocks. Table 5 shows the earnings in per cent of value of stocks listed on the New York Stock Exchange from 1871 to 1937. It can be seen that there is little indication of a trend here although considerable fluctuation took place.

TABLE 5*

EARNINGS RATIOS OF COMMON STOCKS
(PER CENT)

Period	Yield
1871–1880	8.8
1881–1890	6.2
1891–1900	6.2
1901–1910	7.5
1911–1920	10.3
1921–1930	8.01
1931–1937	4.03

* Alfred Cowles, *Common Stock Indexes, Cowles Commission Monograph No. 3* (Bloomington, Ill.: Principia Press, 1938).

Bond yields fell somewhat in this period. Table 6 shows Macaulay's index of the yield of Railroad bonds for the period 1871–1936. It is notable, however, that all of the fall took place in the first decade of the period. We cannot explain much of a trend in saving on that basis.

TABLE 6*

RAILROAD BOND YIELDS

Period	Yield
1871–1880	5.55
1881–1890	3.90
1891–1900	3.49
1901–1910	3.50
1911–1920	4.18
1921–1930	4.43
1931–1936	3.80

* Frederick R. Macaulay, *Bond Yields, Interest Rates and Stock Prices* (New York: National Bureau of Economic Research, 1938).

Railroad bonds are not, of course, perfectly representative of all bonds but they are sufficiently representative to establish the proposition that no very strong trend in long-term interest rates can be observed. That being the case, we cannot explain changes in saving on the basis of changes in the ratio of assets to income or on the basis of changes in the terms on which present income can be traded for future income. That does not mean that those factors cannot influence saving, it only means that during the period 1870 to 1930 they did not move enough actually to affect saving.

11. CHANGES IN TIME PREFERENCE

We now have to consider the problem of inter-temporal changes in time preference. Here we are almost in terra incognita. It is almost impossible to say whether people put a relatively greater value on the future or not. On the one hand the income motive for saving has probably weakened. Whether it is true or not it is generally believed that the chances of making a success of an independent business have grown progressively smaller. The incentive to save in order to found a business is probably weaker on this account. If the income motive ever had any force it was probably based on the possibility of setting up a business. The chances of getting rich by compound interest have never been very good.

On the other hand the security motives for saving are probably stronger than formerly. People who save substantial amounts are not the ones who have to worry about unemployment (at least they did not until the 1930's); but they do have to worry about old age and about supporting their dependents. The weakening of family ties which appears to have taken place requires people to provide their own security against old age and death. Formerly people could place more reliance on children or relatives as a protection against loss of income. The growth of life insurance sales is probably an indication of the increasing strength of security factors in saving.

The growth of life insurance has an independent effect on saving. Saving can only take place when people resist impulses to increase expenditures. A life insurance contract makes such control more effective, for failure to save enough to pay the premium causes the insurance to lapse, which involves considerable loss. The same considerations apply to various contributory pension and annuity plans.

12. CONCLUSIONS

We have shown that the hypothesis developed in Chapter III is consistent with the evidence from budget studies and the income aspiration study. With respect to the long-term movements of saving the problem is more complicated. Our hypothesis can be considered consistent with the data if factors other than income did not have much influence on saving. It is not necessary to show that the non-income factors had no influence. It is only necessary to show that, on balance, those factors could not have changed the savings ratio by more than (say) 5 percentage points. If that is true, our hypothesis explains the data and the alternative hypothesis (that the savings ratio rises with income) does not.

We showed that there is no evidence in support of the idea that introduction of new goods reduces saving. Urbanization may have reduced the savings ratio by (say) 1.5 percentage points. On the other hand, the increase in the rate of growth of income worked in the opposite direction, as did increasing insecurity and the growth of contractual saving. The savings ratio was probably somewhat reduced by the decline in the income motive for saving. Finally, changes in expectations, interest rates, and age distribution appear to have had little effect.

On balance, then, trend factors cannot have had very much influence. We can conclude that our hypothesis is consistent with the data while the alternative is not.

CHAPTER V

SHORT-RUN FLUCTUATIONS IN SAVING[1]

THUS FAR we have considered only long-period variations in saving. Over a period of fifty or seventy-five years the dominant influences on saving are the slow increase in incomes and the equally slow movements of interest rates, expectations, and time preference parameters. If we ask why the savings ratio did not rise appreciably from 1880 to 1930 we have to center our attention on those slowly moving factors. For such a problem it is not illegitimate to neglect short-period changes in income and other factors.

Now, however, we must turn our attention to the explanation of short-run variations in saving. Most of the literature on the consumption function has been devoted to the explanation of variations in saving over relatively short periods. Reasonably accurate yearly data on savings and income are available only for the period since 1919 (indeed the revised Commerce Department data go back only to 1929). Since most consumption function studies have been based on regression methods, attention has been largely confined to the variations in saving during the two decades for which satisfactory data are available. But regressions based on short-period data have been given a long-period interpretation. It has generally been assumed that a regression between saving and income indicates what the long-period consumption function would be in the absence of trend factors. The significance of this interpretation can be understood by a consideration of the forecasts of postwar con-

[1] The substance of this chapter originally appeared in *Income, Employment and Public Policy; Essays in Honor of Alvin H. Hansen* (New York, 1948). It is reprinted here by permission of W. W. Norton & Company, Inc.

sumption made at the end of the war. A number of writers[2] estimated the rate of savings which would obtain if full employment was achieved. It was estimated that full employment real income after the war would be about 40 per cent higher than any income achieved in the twenties or thirties. Some writers took the regression between savings and income from the data of the period 1923–1940 and used it to estimate savings at the higher levels of income expected to rule after the war. These estimates were much too high.[3] We shall try to show that this was so because cyclical fluctuations in income have an effect on saving which is entirely different in character from the effect of secular increases in income.

Most of the articles on the consumption function present hypotheses about the relation between consumption, income, and some other variable such as time, the price level, or the degree of unemployment. The hypothesis is presented in the form of an equation which makes consumption a function of the other variables. The appropriate regression is fitted to the data, and the correlation between the observed and calculated values of consumption or saving is computed. The correlation is invariably high, and most writers seem to be satisfied that a high correlation coefficient provides an adequate test of their hypothesis. But a test which is passed by so many different hypotheses is not a very satisfactory one. Before any more consumption functions are introduced it seems desirable to give some consideration to our methods of testing hypotheses.

In Section 1 it is shown that aggregate hypotheses cannot be adequately tested by the use of correlation analysis. The general principles on which appropriate testing methods can be developed are then discussed. Section 2 is devoted to a consideration of the possibility that the relation between saving and income is different at different points of the trade cycle. A test based on the principles developed in Section 1 shows that we must reject the hypothesis that the savings-income relation is

[2] A. Smithies, "Forecasting Postwar Demand I," *Econometrica* (January 1945).

J. Mosak, "Forecasting Postwar Demand III," *Econometrica* (January 1945).

[3] That is still true even when the regression is based on the revised Commerce Department data.

invariant with respect to measures of position in the trade cycle.

In Section 3 hypotheses which explain both cyclical and secular movements of savings are developed. It is shown that these hypotheses are consistent with (1) the long-run data on income and consumption given by Kuznets, (2) the annual data on income and consumption in the period 1929–1940, (3) the budget study data collected in 1935–36 and 1941. These hypotheses lead to the conclusion that aggregate saving out of disposable income can be estimated by the equation $s_t/y_t = 0.25\ y_t/y_0 - 0.196$ (s_t = current savings, y_t = current disposable income, y_0 = highest disposable income ever attained, all the variables are corrected for population and price changes).

1. Methods of Testing Aggregate Hypotheses

When we deal with a problem in aggregate economics we usually seek for relationships which are, in some sense, invariant. By invariance we do not mean a simple historical invariance like the Pareto law. Rather, we mean that the relationship among a certain set of variables is unaffected by changes in some other variables. The concept of an invariant relationship is therefore a relative one; a relation may be invariant with respect to one set of variables but not with respect to some others. Indeed it might be said that hardly any economic relationship can be regarded as completely invariant. For no economic relation is likely to continue to hold good both before and after a fundamental change in social organization. In fact one of the objects of economic policy is the modification of social organization in such a way as to produce relations of a desirable type among economic variables.

Our idea of invariance is somewhat as follows: We conceive that at any one moment certain variables within the control of households or firms are related in a definite way to certain other variables not within their control. For example, we suppose that the consumption expenditure of families depends on their income. The form of these relations is governed by the behavior characteristics of individuals and by institutional factors such as laws or customs. The relations we seek are invariant with respect to all variables except these psychological or institutional factors. A relation which satisfies that criterion may be said to be more or less stable according as these factors are more or less constant. We can make satisfactory predictions if we can find invariant relations of this type which are highly stable.[4]

If an invariant relation of this type holds for the variables associated with individual households or firms, then a corresponding invariant relation must hold among some functions (not necessarily sums) of all the household or firm variables of the same kind. If we can write $y_i = f_i(x_i)$, for every household (when x_i and y_i are variables applying to the ith household), then we can write $\varphi(x_1, x_2, \ldots, x_n, y_1, y_2, \ldots, y_n) = 0$. The invariance of the second relation will depend on the constancy of the behavior characteristics and institutional elements which determine the invariance of the original relations. Aggregate relations which can be deduced from household or firm relations I shall call fundamental aggregate relations. (There are of course some additional fundamental aggregate relations

---

[4] Finding invariant relations of this sort actually helps in only one kind of policy problem. We may conceive of the "structure" of the economy as being described by a certain set of invariant relations. Then one kind of policy consists in fixing the values of certain of the variables which enter into these equations without otherwise disturbing any of the relations. Fixing an interest rate or tax rate is a policy of this sort. If we know all the invariant relations necessary to describe the structure we can predict the effect of this sort of policy (at least in the sense that we can assign a probability to any values of any economic variable at each point in the future).

On the other hand, many of the most important policies involve changes in the structure. If a law is changed which has never been changed before, then we may know that certain structural equations will be changed but we may not be able to foretell exactly what the new equations will be like. Or, to take a simple example, if the Treasury undertakes a campaign to get people to save more, it will be difficult to know what its effects will be. For this is an attempt to induce changes in behavior patterns and we have comparatively little experience with this kind of change. The kind of data with which economists deal is not likely to reveal anything about the possible effects of the Treasury's campaign. On the other hand, a sufficiently general theory of behavior ought to make a prediction possible but this would be entirely a question of social psychology.

As a matter of fact, it seems probable that most of the economic policies of really fundamental importance involve structural changes of this sort. To the extent that this is true, economists can be regarded as competent to judge the effect of these policies only by default on the part of the social psychologists.

which are definitional and need not be deduced from anything.)

Now consider a pair of such fundamental aggregate relations:

(1) $\varphi_1(x_1, x_2 \ldots, x_n) = \psi_1(y_1, y_2 \ldots, y_n)$

(2) $\varphi_2(x_1, x_2 \ldots, x_n) = \psi_2(z_1, z_2 \ldots, z_n)$ where the x's are exogeneous variables.

It is clear that a further relation

$$(3) \quad \chi_1(y_1, y_2, \ldots, y_n) = \chi_2(z_1, z_2, \ldots z_n)$$

may often follow from the first two and the original household relations. Further, this relation will be invariant so long as (1) and (2) are invariant. This type of relation I shall call a derived aggregate relation.[5]

Now suppose that we observe the historical invariance of the relation (3) and conclude that it is a fundamental relation. We might then conclude that by changing the z's we could manipulate the y's. But we might find instead that we had merely invalidated the relation 2 without having any effect at all on the y's or x's. Derived relations like (3) may break down either as a consequence of policy changes or of structural changes in the economy. In addition there is an important class of derived relations which is likely to hold good only during the course of a single trade cycle. For example, a certain variable z may be partly dependent on the level of unemployment. Within the course of a single trade cycle, income is very closely associated with the level of unemployment. If we have data covering only a single trade cycle, we might conclude from the empirical evidence that z is determined by income. Actually we have a derived relation between z and income, which is bound to break up because the upward trend in income will ultimately change the association between income and unemployment. It is clear from these considerations that many of the relations observed empirically may be only derived relations which will break down because of a structural change in one of the fundamental relations on which they are based. This is particularly true of relations whose existence has been tested against the data of

[5] Cf. T. Haavelmo, "The Probability Approach to Econometrics," *Econometrica* (July 1944), Supplement.

only a single trade cycle. Whether we are concerned with policy or with prediction, we shall often make errors if we treat derived relations as though they were fundamental ones. The difficulty of distinguishing between these two kinds of relations is one of the fundamental difficulties of testing economic hypotheses.

Let us now return to a consideration of the adequacy of correlation methods of hypothesis testing. Suppose we have a hypothesis which asserts that total consumer expenditure is dependent on disposable income. We can fit a regression to the data for income and consumption and compute the correlation coefficient. When we find a significant correlation, what, exactly, have we found? We have merely disproved the null hypothesis. That is, we have shown that the "association" between income and consumption was too strong to allow us to ascribe it to chance. Then we should be reasonably confident in asserting that we had found either, (a) a fundamental relation between income and consumption or, (b) a derived relation between them, or (c) evidence of lack of randomness such as the null hypothesis assumes. We might exploit our results a little further. If it could be shown that the lower confidence limit on the correlation was (say) .95, we could assert that during the period income was linearly related to all the variables fundamentally related to consumption. But this is about as far as we can safely go. It can be argued, of course, that a derived relation will tend to produce lower correlations than a fundamental relation. But, when our data cover only short periods, the connections between economic variables may be so close that the differences in correlations between the two sorts of relations may be too small to be statistically significant. Moreover, if the variables in a derived relation have a lower observational error than those in the fundamental relations, the correlation in the derived relation may be the higher one.

A very simple example of a derived relation is that which appears to have existed between consumer expenditures in dollars and disposable income in dollars during the period 1929–1940. Just as good a correlation is obtained by using undeflated as deflated data. This can only be true because the price level was related to income during the period. If real consumption is fundamentally related to real income, the money relationship is a derived one and will break down in the postwar period unless prices continue to be related to income in the prewar fashion. Conversely, if money consumption is fundamentally related to money income, the relation between the real variables is a derived one and will break down. Now it is obviously of vital importance to know which is the fundamental relation, but the correlation test is not very helpful.

The difficulties we have just been discussing arise because of the existence of derived relations among aggregate variables. But, ordinarily, such derived relations will not hold for individual firms or households. This suggests that in testing hypotheses we ought to operate on the following principles. First, every hypothesis ought to be stated in terms of the behavior of individual firms or households, even when we are only interested in aggregate results. This does not, of course, prevent us from considering interactions among individuals any more than the use of the theory of the firm in analysis of monopolistic competition prevents us from dealing with interactions among firms. Second, in so far as it is possible, we ought to test our hypotheses against data which indicate the behavior of individual households or firms. This does not mean that we ought to abandon statistical procedures. Nearly every hypothesis has to allow for random elements in behavior so that in making tests we have to measure the average behavior of groups. But by dealing with relatively small groups we may sometimes escape the net of interrelations which makes it impossible to test aggregate hypotheses.

Suppose we are faced with the following situation. One hypothesis asserts that saving varies with income and the price level, another asserts that saving depends on income alone. Aggregate income and the price level are related in the period for which data are available. Then if one of these hypotheses is true, it will be impossible to disprove the other by means of aggregate data alone. But, while movements of aggregate income may have been correlated with those of the price level, there are certainly some similar individuals whose incomes moved in a different way. By studying the behavior of those individuals it will be possible to disprove one of the hypotheses. When this has been done the parameters in the chosen relation may be fitted by the use of aggregate data (though in some cases this may still be difficult because of multicollinearity).

Of course it will not always be possible to find the data necessary to test every hypothesis. But there is a great deal of microeconomic data which has never been properly exploited because of the tendency of econometricians to emphasize parameter fitting rather than hypothesis testing. Actually it is much more important to work with a true hypothesis than to make extremely precise estimates of parameters.

2. SAVING DEPENDS ON PAST AS WELL AS CURRENT INCOME

In this section we shall apply the method just suggested to some questions about the consumption function. In the view of a number of writers, notably Smithies and Mosak,[6] consumer expenditures are essentially dependent on disposable income. The effect on consumption of an increase in income is supposed to be the same whether the increase comes about through a rise of employment during the recovery from a depression or through a rise in productivity in a period of sustained full employment like that of the twenties. Professor Hansen[7] and Professor Samuelson[8] have maintained for some time that the relation between income and consumption varies through the trade cycle. Mr. Woytinski[9] and Mr. Bean[10] have made similar statements and have tried to test them empirically. They obtained correlations just as good as the others but no better, and certainly cannot claim to have disproved the alternative hy-

[6] "Forecasting Postwar Demand, I, III," *Econometrica* (January 1945).

[7] *Fiscal Policy and Business Cycles* (New York: W. W. Norton & Company, Inc., 1941), pp. 225–249.

[8] "Full Employment after the War," in *Postwar Economic Problems,* edited by S. E. Harris (New York: McGraw-Hill Book Company, Inc., 1943).

[9] "Relationship between Consumers' Expenditures, Savings and Disposable Income," *Review of Economic Statistics* (January 1946).

[10] Louis Bean, "Relation of Disposable Income and the Business Cycle to Expenditures," *Review of Economic Statistics* (November 1946).

pothesis. There is, however, some evidence which proves nearly conclusively that the consumption function is cyclically variable though not quite in the ways suggested by Bean or Woytinski.

This evidence is provided by the budget studies made in 1935–36 and 1941. One of the remarkable results of the Study of Consumer Purchases of 1935–36 was that a great number of families reported expenditures in excess of income for the year. The average deficit of the under $500 a year group amounted to 50 per cent of income while the average deficit of the $500–$1000 group was 10 per cent of income.[11] The results of the 1935–36 study are not above criticism, of course, but the fact that deficits were reported in every city and every area, together with the independent evidence of studies like those of Bakke, Gilboy, Clague and Powell,[12] makes it clear that very substantial deficits did occur during the depression.

The total deficits of urban and rural non-farm, white, non-relief families alone amounted to 593 million dollars. Since total net savings of consumers during the thirties varied from $1.4 to $3.7 billion, an explanation of the deficits can contribute a good deal to our understanding of variations in saving.

But the real significance of the deficits does not lie in their magnitude but in what they reveal about the relations between income and saving. Let us first consider what kind of people were in the low-income groups in 1935–36. While there is little direct information about the low-income families in 1935–36, a rough estimate of their composition can be made from the data on income and employment in 1939 contained in the Census of 1940. Table 7 shows the result of this estimate.

In the nature of the case this estimate can be only a rough one since it had to be based on a number of unverified assump-

---

[11] National Resources Committee, *Family Expenditures in the United States.*

[12] E. W. Bakke, *The Unemployed Worker* (New Haven: Yale University Press, 1940).

Ewan Clague and W. Powell, *Ten Thousand Out of Work* (Philadelphia: University of Pennsylvania Press, 1933).

E. W. Gilboy, *Applicants for Work Relief* (Cambridge: Harvard University Press, 1940).

TABLE 7

WHITE URBAN AND RURAL NON-FARM FAMILIES WITH
INCOME UNDER $1000 IN 1935–36

	Relief	Non-Relief
Retired...............................	600,000	600,000
Independent Business and Professional...	100,000	600,000
Partially or Fully Unemployed..........	2,100,000	1,900,000
Fully Employed.......................	...	2,400,000
Total.........................	2,800,000	5,500,000

tions. Yet there does not seem to be much doubt that the non-relief low-income families included a high proportion of families whose incomes were low because of unemployment and whose incomes were much higher in periods of full employment. Moreover, some of the families in the independent business and professional group would have higher incomes in more prosperous periods. Finally, some of the fully employed wage and salary workers were down-graded from higher wage jobs so that their normal incomes were higher than the income reported in 1935–36.

Keeping these considerations in mind let us now ask what is the significance of the deficits for the theory of saving. A supporter of the view that saving depends on real income would say, presumably, that $c/y = f(y)$ and that c/y exceeds 1 for some positive value of y. When that value of y is reached those who have assets or credit will have deficits, the others will have to be content with spending all of their income.

In its simple form this position is untenable. For the breakeven point (the income at which consumption just equals income) stood at about $800 in 1941 prices in 1917.[13] In 1935–36 the breakeven point stood at about $1500 in 1941 prices. If consumption were merely a function of current income the breakeven level of income should have remained the same. To

[13] Bean, "Relation of Disposable Income and the Business Cycle."

this the sophisticated Keynesian will reply by introducing a trend factor. Consumption at a given level of income can be changed by the introduction of new goods (this is about the only factor likely to cause a trend in the consumption of urban families and these are the families included in the budget studies in question). For the sake of the argument let us agree that introduction of new goods in itself increases consumption at a given level of income. We know too that families in the low-income groups were driving automobiles and using various recently introduced household appliances. This does not advance the argument much, however, for the families in question were for the most part using these things rather than buying them. We can turn to other new goods, movies and silk stockings (say), which were also consumed by the low-income groups in the thirties. Let us grant that a family with an $800 income did not buy these things in 1917 and did in 1935 (and neglect the possibility that purchases of these goods represented substitution rather than additional consumption). Then it follows that at least part of the deficits in the thirties were due to the fact that low-income families bought new goods which did not exist in the earlier period. But this is not the whole story. We can say on the one hand that families at an $800 income level in the thirties spent more than families with that income in 1917 because they had become used to a high standard of living (including silk stockings and movies) in the twenties and found it difficult to give up. Or we can say that even if income had remained constant from 1917 to 1935 the attraction of these new goods was so irresistible that they incurred deficits to get them (or at least that they would have done so if they had the necessary assets or credit). The latter position seems to be a somewhat untenable one. But if we argue that consumption depends on current real income and trend, that is the position which must be maintained in order to explain the facts. For if we write $c = f(y,t)$ nothing has been said about the influence of past living standards on current consumption.

This does not disprove the proposition that consumption at a given moment is dependent on real income alone but it does require the supporters of that proposition to subscribe to some very strong propositions about the influence of new products and similar trend factors.

We can make a further test if we compare the deficits reported in 1935–36 with those reported in 1941. Deficits at given levels of income were much smaller in 1941 than in 1935–36. At every level deficits were less than one-half as great in 1941 as in 1935–36.[14] How is this shift to be explained? Suppose the

CHART II—AVERAGE URBAN MONEY INCOME AND PER CENT SAVED, BASED ON SURVEYS OF 1901, 1917-19, 1935-36, AND 1941

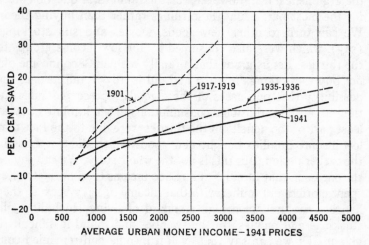

Source, Bean, *op. cit.*

deficits, in both cases, were due to the fact that families whose incomes had fallen as a result of unemployment found it hard to reduce their living standards. Then the explanation is easy. The low-income group consists primarily of two subgroups: families whose earners are normally fully employed at low wages and families whose incomes have been reduced by unemployment. The second group will run deficits to protect the high living standard attained when they were fully employed. The first group balances its budget. Suppose now that we have com-

[14] U. S. Bureau of Labor Statistics *Bulletin* 724. See also Chart II.

plete data on families in the $1000 income group in two periods. Suppose that the situation is as follows:

	Number	*Deficit*
Fully Employed Families (with normal incomes)...	5000	0
Partially Employed Families.....................	5000	$300
Average.......................................		$150

Suppose that in a second period we obtain reports from the same group but that half of the families in the $1000 group have increased their incomes. The situation in the $1000 group now is as follows:

	Number	*Deficit*
Fully Employed Families..........	5000	0
Partially Employed Families.......	2500	$300
Average.......................		$100

Now suppose that instead of subdividing the families in this way our report had shown only the average deficit of the $1000 income families. We would have observed a reduction in the average deficit from $150 to $100 per family without knowing why. The difference in the 1935–36 and 1941 studies seems to correspond very clearly to the examples just given. In 1935–36 there were about eight million unemployed; in 1941 there were only three million. In 1935–36 a much higher proportion of families in the low-income groups were there because of unemployment than there were in 1941. If, therefore, we accept the proposition that the deficits were due to unemployment, or to incomes low by comparison with previous ones, the difference between the two studies is easily explained.

If we try to support the view that consumption depends on absolute income how shall we explain the difference? The trend explanation cannot be used in this case. For the breakeven point moves in the wrong direction. (Note, however, that in the upper groups saving at each level of income was lower than in 1935–36. This means that some sort of trend factor was at work but does not explain the deficits. This movement can be explained by the long-run theory of Chapter III.)

We can suppose that the families left in the low-income groups would have liked to run deficits but were unable to do so because they lacked the necessary assets or credit. But we have argued that a higher proportion of the low-income group in 1941 were permanent members of that group than in 1935–36. It follows that the higher deficits in 1935–36 must have been incurred by the group whose incomes had fallen. For those permanently in the low-income group were in more or less the same position in both years. Then we have to explain the differences in the reactions of the two groups. There are three possible explanations. (1) The families with temporarily low incomes were technically in a better position to have deficits. That is, they were not more willing to run deficits but more able to get the resources to do so. (2) The families with temporarily low incomes had expectations of reëmployment and higher income in the future. (3) These families had had higher living standards in the past and were therefore more willing to have deficits to protect their living standards.

If either of the last two factors is influential then consumption must depend on past income (since this governs the expected level of income at full employment) as well as on current income. In this case a general rise in income to levels above the 1929 peak followed by a fall would bring about a recurrence of the deficits. For the standard of living and expectations of income would be based on the new peak. If income declined from this peak by the same percentage as 1935 income had declined from the 1929 peak, deficits of a relative magnitude as large as those of 1935 would occur. This would be true even if the absolute level of income were as high as the 1929 level. On the other hand if the breakeven point is independent of past levels of income no deficits would occur unless income were absolutely low.

The budget study data do not tell us anything directly about which of the three factors just mentioned are actually relevant. We must leave the question open for the moment. However, it should be noted that the hypothesis that consumption depends on past as well as on current income is consistent with all the data discussed so far. The alternative hypothesis that consumption depends only on current income can be made consistent with the data only if we are willing to accept some rather doubtful subsidiary propositions.

One further piece of evidence is available for testing these two hypotheses. The 1941 budget study reported income for the first quarter of 1942 as well as for 1941. Families at each income level were classified by the changes in their income. Savings for the first quarter of 1942 were separately reported for those whose incomes had increased more than 5 per cent, and those whose incomes had decreased more than 5 per cent from the 1941 level. The results are shown in Table 8. Families whose incomes rose had about the same savings or deficits as those whose incomes stayed the same. On the other hand,

TABLE 8

AVERAGE YEARLY SAVINGS FOR CITY FAMILIES BY INCOME CHANGE
FROM 1941 TO 1942

Money Income Class in 1942	Consumers Whose Incomes in 1942		
	Decreased over 5%	Changed less than 5%	Increased over 5%
0 to $1000..............	−337	−35	−15
$1000 to $1500..............	−181	−34	62
$1500 to $2000..............	−81	126	157
$2000 to $3000..............	0	242	290
$3000 and over.............	143	1228	1059

Annual rate for 1942 based on first quarter.
Based on B. L. S. *Bulletin* 724.

families whose incomes fell had much smaller savings or larger deficits than those whose incomes stayed constant.

Now these facts can be interpreted in two ways. On the one hand we can say that they show that a rate of change factor is important in the determination of saving. That is, we write $c/y = f(y,y')$ where y' is the rate of change of income. On the other hand we can say that saving is low when income is low relative to past income. The two explanations are not the same. In a year when income is declining, either explanation would lead to the same result. But suppose that income declines and then remains at a (more or less constant) low level. After the decline has stopped the rate of change is zero but income is still low relative to its pre-depression levels.

It is fairly easy to tell which of the two hypotheses is correct. If the rate of change of income is an important factor it should show up in regressions of aggregate data. But it is well known that when the equation $c = f(y, t, y')$ is fitted to aggregate data for the twenties and thirties the addition of the factor y' contributes very little to the correlation. In the face of the budget study data this is difficult to explain unless we accept relative income instead of rate of change as the explanation of the differences in saving at the same level of income.

The asymmetry in the results is also important. If we take the view that rate of change of income is a determinate of saving then there are strong reasons for supposing that the adjustment lag works in both directions. On the other hand, if we argue that people whose incomes are low relative to their past incomes reduce saving to protect their living standard, the asymmetry is easy to understand. Those whose incomes rose were for the most part getting back to levels of incomes which they had previously experienced. In these circumstances they merely return to the expenditure patterns of the past and no adjustment lag is involved.

The data just discussed seem to show fairly conclusively that consumption at a given level of income does depend on past income. This hypothesis is consistent with the existence of deficits in 1935–36 and 1941, with the changes in deficits (at given levels of income) from 1935–36 to 1941, with the upward movement of the breakeven point from 1901 and 1917 to 1935–36 and 1941, and with the differences in saving among families whose incomes had changed in different ways. It is difficult to explain all of these facts on any other hypothesis.

So far our argument has been a strictly empirical one. But it must be clear that it also has a strong psychological foundation. The fundamental psychological postulate underlying our argument is that it is harder for a family to reduce its expenditures from a high level than for a family to refrain from making high expenditures in the first place. Consider two families who have incomes of $1000 a year at a particular time. Now suppose one of these families has an income of $1000 per year for ten years thereafter. Suppose the other family gets an increase in income from $1000 to $1500, retains this position for nine years, and then has its income reduced to $1000 so that in the last year it is in the same position as the other family. Initially both families might have exactly balanced their budgets at $1000 and the first family might continue in this way for the whole ten-year period. But when the second family had its income increased it would increase its consumption by (say) $400 and its saving by $100. When the reduction in income occurred this family would certainly find it difficult to cut its consumption to the $1000 level. The first family had only to refrain from increasing its consumption expenditures to balance its budget. The second family had actually to give up consumption of $400 per year to achieve the same result. It would be surprising if a family in these circumstances succeeded in reducing its consumption sufficiently to balance its budget after the loss in income.

Since all of the data are consistent with the view that this does happen, there does not seem to be much doubt that past income has an influence on current consumption and saving.

The argument so far has been devoted to explaining the deficits reported in the budget studies. But the significant result of this argument is not the conclusion that deficits will occur when income falls below previously attained levels, but the more general proposition that families are willing to sacrifice saving in order to protect their living standard. This proposition applies to all income groups who have suffered losses in income. We can argue in the following way. If a family has a certain income y_0 and this income is higher than any previously attained it will save some amount. This amount will be a function of income $s_0 = f(y_0)$. If its income increases the same function will hold. But if, after an increase, income falls to the original level, its saving will be less than $f(y_0)$. If the family's income and saving are low throughout it will have a deficit after the fall in income. If the familly is in a higher bracket it will simply save less after the fall in income than it did before the increase.

We have now shown that consumption is dependent on current income relative to past income as well as on the absolute level of current income. The problem now is to find just which past incomes are relevant. In view of the argument just given, we appear safe in supposing that past incomes lower than the current one are not very relevant. This is pretty well demonstrated by the 1941-42 budget figures cited above. Families whose incomes rose to a given level saved about the same amount as those whose incomes had been at that level in the previous year. At first glance then it would seem reasonable to suppose that current consumption depends on the ratio of current income to some weighted average of past higher incomes with weights decreasing as the time interval involved grows longer. There are, however, some fairly strong arguments against this position.

The declines in income which occur in the depression are not uniformly distributed even though the size distribution of income remains more or less unchanged. Income losses will be of three kinds, (1) reductions in property incomes, (2) reductions in wage rates, (3) losses due to underemployment. Since real wage rates do not decline very much in the depression (and were even higher in the late years of the depression than in the twenties) losses of income are mostly of types (1) and (3). (A fourth class results from down-grading of workers either within or between industries but for our purposes this can be regarded as underemployment.)

Let us first consider the effect of losses of income in the upper-income groups. It is not important here whether the losses are due to reductions in property incomes or to salary reductions. It can be assumed, however, that unemployment among the upper-income groups is not important. The upper 10 per cent of the income distribution produces almost all of the positive saving for the whole economy. Moreover, families in this group save a high proportion of their income. This means that they have a good deal of leeway in maintaining consumption standards without running into deficits. When high-income families suffer a loss in income, therefore, they continue to live in the same kind of neighborhoods and maintain their contacts with others of the same socio-economic status. In general they maintain the way of life which was established before the onset of the depression. They will, of course, cut expenditures on some lines, particularly on durable goods. But in view of the high rate of savings maintained in prosperity they can absorb a considerable reduction of income by reducing saving without cutting consumption too deeply. Moreover, there is no reason why they should not continue in this position for several years. Suppose now that income falls sharply from a cyclical peak and then remains constant for several years. The peak year's consumption sets the standard from which cuts are made (provided the peak did not represent a mere spurt in income). The higher the peak consumption the more difficult it will be to reduce consumption to any given level. After the initial reductions are made the situation becomes static. The peak year does not lose its influence because the consumption of the following years depends on the peak consumption. Of course, if income began to fall again, further consumption cuts would take place and the intermediate level of income would be important in determining the extent of the cuts as well as the previous peak income. But if the depression consists in a fall of income lasting only a couple of years followed by a rise or a low plateau, the consumption of the peak year is likely to have very heavy weight in determining consumption in the depression. The influence of the peak consumption will not "fade away" unless income continues to fall steadily.

All of the above argument applies only to the upper-income groups. Those who were in the lower 90 per cent of the distribution in prosperity are in a different situation. For this group reductions in income are usually associated with unemployment. (These people probably save very little even in prosperous times.) In a depression they can only influence saving by having deficits. A considerable number of families in this group go nearly unscathed by the depression. Their real wages do not fall and they never have serious losses of employment. These we may leave out of account since their savings are simply zero throughout. The remaining families suffer serious loss of employment at some point during the depression. These may also be divided into two groups. Some will remain employed up to a certain point, then lose their jobs and never get steady employment again until a high level of prosperity is reached. These families will presumably run substantial deficits immediately after they become unemployed, but as their assets become smaller they will have to adjust to the new situation and presumably balance budgets in which relief is the principal source of income. They may continue to have deficits for a long time but in any case the influence of the prosperity living standards will certainly "fade away" as time passes. However, it should be noted that not all of the persons who will eventually constitute the "hard core" of unemployment get there at once. The result is that a certain number of families are going through the initial stages of long-term unemployment at any time during the depression. Presumably, however, there are rather more families in this position during the downturn in the early years than later on. We should expect, therefore, to find somewhat greater deficits and lower aggregate savings at a given income in the downturn than in the upturn. However, the total number of families in this group was not very large in the thirties and the differences in the numbers entering cannot have been great enough to cause numerically important reductions in aggregate savings.

The remainder of the unemployment is widely spread so that a large number of workers "take turns" being unemployed. Families lose income through unemployment and accordingly cut consumption but also run a deficit. When they become reemployed they may return to something very close to the prosperity consumption standard. Sometimes later unemployment recurs and the process repeats. Those families who are very frequently in and out of employment will presumably gradually reduce consumption (even when employed) because of the decrease in their assets and the accumulation of debt. The influence of the peak standard will therefore gradually lose its effect.

But a great part of the total unemployment can be accounted for by families who have only two or three stretches of prolonged unemployment during the depression. For those families the influence of the peak consumption standard will not fade away because it renews itself with each stretch of full employment.

We can conclude then that the income or consumption of the last cyclical peak will carry a special and very heavy weight in determining consumption at a given (lower) level of income during a depression. In principle a weighted average of all the incomes from the peak year to the current year ought to be used. But with only a few observations it would be impossible to estimate the weights. In what follows we shall consider the relation of current consumption to the ratio of current income to highest previously attained income, but the results are to be taken as an approximation to the true relation.

If the argument just given is correct, there is a cyclical component in the explanation of saving. Savings at a given level of income, when income is the highest ever attained, as in the late twenties, will be higher than savings at a similar income level reached in a decline from a still higher level. I conclude, therefore, that in a general way at least the propositions of those who have argued that saving varies with the trade cycle as well as with income are supported by the evidence of the budget studies.

3. SECULAR AND CYCLICAL MOVEMENTS OF THE SAVINGS RATIO

So far it has been shown that saving depends on the level of current incomes relative to higher incomes in previous years. But saving also depends on the absolute level of income. We may write then, $S_t = f(y_t, y_t/y_0)$ where y_0 is the highest income attained previous to the year t.

If data covering a number of cycles were available, we could take the regression of saving on y_t/y_0 and y_t and estimate simultaneously the secular and cyclical components in saving. Unfortunately the period 1929–1940 covers less than one major cycle so that we are forced to estimate the influence of the two factors separately. However, as we have already shown, there are strong grounds for believing that (in the absence of cyclical fluctuations) the relation between aggregate saving and aggregate income is one of proportionality.

If the secular relation between saving and consumption is one of proportionality the *proportion* of income saved will depend only on cyclical factors. Then we may write $S_t/y_t = F(y_t/y_0)$. If a linear approximation yields a good fit it can safely be used for projections. For the variations in y_t/y_0 are not likely to exceed those which occurred during the period 1929–1940. When the relation $s_t/y_t = a(y_t/y_0) + b$ is fitted to the data for that period we obtain $a = 0.25$, $b = 0.196$. The correlation is 0.9 which is as good as that usually obtained for relations between savings and income.[15]

However, the correlation is not the test of the adequacy of our hypothesis. The real tests are (1) the budget study data already discussed, and (2) the success of predictions based on our regression. The regression combines two hypotheses. The one given in the last two chapters, i.e., that cet. par. savings tend to be proportional to income in the long-run and the short-run hypothesis discussed in this chapter. If these hypotheses are correct we should be able to predict the savings ratio from our equation. Since we used only a short period in getting the regression we can make predictions both forward and backward.

If we substitute $Y_t/Y_0 = 1.03$ in our equation we get an estimate of the savings ratio which should obtain in a period of slowly rising income. Making the substitution we obtain .06 for our estimate. As we have already shown, the Kuznets data show that in the period 1880–1930 personal savings were somewhat less than 10 per cent. (We cannot make a more accurate statement than that since we can only guess at the extent of Kuznets' overestimate.) Our "prediction" then cannot be very far off. The facts are not inconsistent with our hypothesis to any serious extent. It will be noted that we did not use any data from the

---

[15] The computations are based on the income and savings data in the July 1947 Supplement to *The Survey of Current Business*. The data were put on a per capita basis and deflated by the B. L. S. consumer price index.

prediction period to get our equation. There is, therefore, no objection to projecting it backward.

We can also make a test by means of a forward prediction. If 1947 can be considered a normal year we can see how our formula works in predicting savings for that year. Taking 1947 real income per capita at 5 per cent below 1946, we put $Y_t/Y_0 =$ 0.95. Our estimate of the 1947 savings ratio is then 4.1 per cent. The actual figure was 5.1 per cent. If 1947 can be considered a

TABLE 9

ACTUAL AND ESTIMATED SAVINGS AS PER CENT OF DISPOSABLE INCOME

Year	Estimated	Actual	Estimated—Actual
1929	5.4	4.3	1.1
1930	2.9	3.8	−.9
1931	1.4	2.8	−1.4
1932	−2.1	−2.9	.8
1933	−2.3	−2.6	.3
1934	−0.6	−0.4	−.2
1935	1.9	3.0	−1.1
1936	4.7	5.1	−.4
1937	4.7	5.3	−.6
1938	3.2	1.5	1.7
1939	4.7	3.7	1.0
1940	6.2	4.7	1.5
1941	9.2	10.3	−1.1

normal year and if non-income factors were unchanged from before the war, our prediction is a success. Unfortunately there is some doubt on both counts.

Some consumer goods were still in short supply in 1947. This might be expected to increase the savings ratio. Income was somewhat more equally distributed, which would ordinarily be expected to reduce the savings ratio (in the short run). However, much of the gain of the lower-income groups went to farmers who tend to save more than others. The net effect of the change in the size distribution was probably small. In addition, however, a great many rank shifts took place. Rentiers and salaried workers faced losses in income through the inflation while others gained. In general the effect of rank shifts will be adverse to saving. People whose incomes fall probably cut their saving by more than those who gain.

Finally there are asset and income expectations. The increase in private holdings of government bonds and bank deposits was more than proportional to the increase in income since the beginning of the war. On the other hand, the sluggishness of the stock market kept private security assets from rising in proportion to income. On balance the change in the ratio of assets to income was probably not very great but it may have had some effect. Income expectation factors were probably favorable to saving since predictions of a depression were common during much of 1947.

Thus shortages and income expectations probably worked to increase savings while rank shifts in income and asset effects probably worked in the opposite direction. There is no reason to suppose that these factors balanced out. We can only say that our hypothesis produced a successful prediction. That success may or may not have been invalidated by the factors just discussed. A real test will come when a few more years have passed.

CHAPTER VI

THE IMPLICATIONS OF INTERDEPENDENT PREFERENCES

OUR CRITIQUE of the theory of saving is also a critique of the general theory of consumer behavior. We have shown that the interdependence of consumer preferences affects the choice between consumption and saving to an important extent. But if that is true other choices will also be affected, choices between leisure and income, or between different kinds of current expenditure.

Development of a complete theory of consumers' choice on the assumption of interdependent preferences is beyond the scope of the present work. But our task would be incomplete if we did not give some indication of the character of such a theory. This chapter therefore contains two examples of the way in which economic theory is affected by the interdependence of preferences.

1. SOME WELFARE CONSIDERATIONS

Since the rediscovery of the work of Pareto and Barone and the independent work of Lerner and Hotelling there has been a revival of interest in the field of Welfare Economics. By contrast with much earlier work, the "new welfare economics" has been characterized by a consistent attempt to maintain a clear distinction between positive economics and ethics. In particular the utilitarian welfare objective, the maximization of a sum of individual utility indices, has been abandoned. This abandonment of a time-honored concept results from ethical as well as positive considerations. From a positive standpoint there is considerable doubt whether cardinal utility can be measured (even under ideal experimental conditions), since cardinal measurement involves the dubious assumption that the utility of at least one good is independent.[1] On ethical grounds, equality as an independent goal holds a higher place in many people's value systems than formerly, while utilitarianism as a general system of ethics finds few adherents. Since the utilitarian argument for equality was a very thin one, it was abandoned in favor of a position permitting independent judgments about the distribution of income.

In its most general form modern welfare economics can be applied to any ethical system whatever. We require only that the ethical system enable us to judge whether one set of economic (or economically influenced) magnitudes is to be considered better than, worse than, or indifferent to any other set. If it does, we can set up a social welfare index (perfectly analogous to the individual utility index), and this index will be a function of the economic magnitudes and any other variables affected by economic events. Thus we have $w = w(x_1, x_2, \ldots, x_m)$ where the x's are the variables just mentioned.[2]

In addition to the welfare function which expresses an ethical position, we have two sets of relationships among the included variables. These are (1) technological relationships, and (2) the relationships which describe the behavior of the participants in the system under various sets of institutional arrangements. The problem is to maximize the welfare function subject to these restraints. This amounts to choosing from the set of all possible institutional arrangements, that subset which will produce behavior relations yielding the greatest value for W. Even on a given ethical criterion, solutions to the welfare problem will vary widely according to the degree of freedom allowed in the choice of institutional arrangements. If one is a complete determinist, the W function has a uniquely determined value (except for random elements) and there is no problem. On the other hand, a sufficiently revolutionary attitude allows one to

[1] Professor Samuelson has recently shown that the assumption of independence of utilities involves restrictions on demand functions which make the assumption even more doubtful than might be expected from *a priori* considerations. *Foundations of Economic Analysis*, pp. 174 ff.

[2] In this section I have drawn freely on the work of Professor Samuelson; *vide* Samuelson *op. cit.*, chap. viii.

choose almost any conceivable set of institutional arrangements including those which will "change human nature."

So far, all that has been done is to ask the welfare question in a clear-cut way. But, to go farther, we have to put more details into the welfare function and the constraints.

The assumptions usually made are:

(1) The social welfare function is a function of the (ordinal) utility indices of individuals. These in turn are functions of the amounts of goods received and services supplied by the individuals.

$$W = W \ [U^1 \ (X^1{}_1, \ \ldots \ X^1{}_n, V^1{}_1, \ \ldots \ V^1{}_n). \ \ldots$$
$$U^s(X^s{}_1, \ \ldots \ X^s{}_n, V^s{}_1, \ \ldots \ V^s{}_n)]$$

where $X_i{}^j$ and $V_i{}^j$ are the ith good received and service supplied by the jth individual and the U^j is the utility index of individual j. It will be noted that this is an ethical assumption of some consequence. There is a wide range of ethical beliefs which cannot be described in terms of satisfaction of individual preferences, for example, belief in prohibition.

(2) Only the goods received and services supplied by an individual enter into his utility function. Goods received by others are presumed not to affect his utility index.

(3) As I have already indicated, the new welfare economics makes a sharp distinction between positive and ethical propositions—in particular, ethical propositions connected with the distribution of welfare. This is achieved by leaving the welfare function largely unspecified, up to the last possible moment. It is some function of individual utility indices and it is only required that the function increase in value if one of the individual indices increases while the others remain the same or increase. If one individual's welfare increases while another's decreases, the sign of the change in the welfare function is unspecified. From the assumptions just given plus certain familiar assumptions about individual preferences and technological relationships, it is possible to deduce certain relationships which must hold if the welfare function is to be maximized. These conditions must be satisfied regardless of the details of the dis-

tribution ethics underlying the welfare function, provided the ethics are consistent with assumption (1).

These conditions are: (A) The marginal productivity of a given factor in one line is to the marginal productivity of that factor in any other line as the marginal productivity of any other factor in the first line is to the marginal productivity of the second factor in the second line.

(B) The marginal rate of substitution between any two goods must be the same for all individuals; this common rate must equal the rate at which one good can be transformed into another by transferring any resources from production of one good to production of the other.

(C) The marginal rate of substitution between any productive service supplied and any good consumed must be the same for all individuals and must equal the marginal productivity of the service in terms of the good in question.

In the case of a community using money and prices and allowing individuals to choose the goods they will buy and the services they will supply, these conditions can be interpreted in terms of price, cost, and productivity relations. These amount to (a) prices of goods must be the same for all consumers and equal to marginal production costs; (b) the price of any factor must be the same in all uses and equal to the value of its marginal product. Note that factor prices have to be stated net of taxation. It is the net income obtained from supplying more of a service which is relevant to the individual's choice between leisure and goods.

So far we have stated the essential results of the new welfare economics. But these results were obtained on the assumption (2) above, that every individual's preferences are independent of the amount of goods consumed by other individuals. We have already shown that this assumption cannot be considered valid in the light of observation. Our task now is to set out the implications of that fact in terms of the new welfare economics. We shall accept all the assumptions described above except the one about independence of preferences and follow the same procedure in obtaining our results as was used in obtaining the results stated above.

Since our interest will center on the question of the relation between factor prices and productivity, we shall consider a community producing only one commodity with but one production service per person. To simplify our problem we shall suppose the community to consist of three individuals. (The results can be easily generalized to include a larger number.) The utility index of each individual is supposed to depend on the amount of income (in terms of the single commodity) received by him *and* on the amounts received by the others, and finally upon the amount of productive services supplied by him. Denoting the productive services supplied by the three individuals as x_1, x_2, x_3 respectively, their incomes as y_1, y_2, y_3 and their utility indices by u_1, u_2, u_3, we have

$$(1) \qquad u_1 = \phi_1 (x_1, y_1, y_2, y_3)$$

$$(2) \qquad u_2 = \phi_2 (x_2, y_1, y_2, y_3)$$

$$(3) \qquad u_3 = \phi_3 (x_3, y_1, y_2, y_3)$$

If the three kinds of services are used jointly to produce the single commodity we have a production function

$$(4) \qquad y_1 + y_2 + y_3 = \psi (x_1, x_2, x_3).$$

Our problem is to find rules defining the set of all positions having the property that the utility of one individual cannot be increased without decreasing that of another. Regardless of our distributive ethics the social welfare function cannot be a maximum unless that condition is satisfied. In the nature of the situation there must be an infinite set of positions satisfying the conditions and any of them can be chosen on ethical grounds (subject only to institutional restrictions).

To find the rules which must be satisfied to fulfill the objectives just described, we proceed as follows: we first suppose the utility of two of our individuals to be fixed so that we have

$$(1a) \qquad u_1 = \phi_1 (x_1, y_1, y_2, y_3) = \bar{u}_1$$

$$(2a) \qquad u_2 = \phi_2 (x_2, y_1, y_2, y_3) = \bar{u}_2$$

This means that we place the individuals (1) and (2) on given indifference surfaces. Next we find the values of x_1, x_2, x_3, y_1, y_2, y_3 which maximize u_3 subject to conditions 1a and 2a and the production function (4). This means that we find a position such that we cannot increase the utility of (3) without reducing that of (1) or (2). Because of the symmetry of the relationships it does not make any difference whether we fix the utility of (1) and (2) and maximize that of (3) or fix (1) and (3) and maximize (2). The relations we shall obtain will not involve $\bar{u}_1$ or $\bar{u}_2$ but simply define a set of values for the variables which will satisfy the maximum criterion described above.

The method of maximization is exactly that used in obtaining the welfare results for the independence case so I shall give only the results. When we have gone through the maximization, we obtain the following conditions:

(5) $\partial\psi/\partial x_1 =$

$$-\frac{\partial\phi_1/\partial x_1}{R_{11}}\frac{\left[1 - \dfrac{R_{21}}{R_{22}} - \dfrac{R_{31}}{R_{33}} + \dfrac{R_{31}}{R_{33}}\dfrac{R_{33}}{R_{22}} + \dfrac{R_{21}}{R_{22}}\dfrac{R_{32}}{R_{33}} - \dfrac{R_{32}}{R_{33}}\dfrac{R_{23}}{R_{22}}\right]}{D}$$

(6) $\partial\psi/\partial x_2 =$

$$-\frac{\partial\phi_2/\partial x_2}{R_{22}}\frac{\left[1 - \dfrac{R_{12}}{R_{11}} - \dfrac{R_{32}}{R_{33}} + \dfrac{R_{32}}{R_{33}}\dfrac{R_{13}}{R_{11}} + \dfrac{R_{31}}{R_{33}}\dfrac{R_{12}}{R_{11}} - \dfrac{R_{31}}{R_{33}}\dfrac{R_{13}}{R_{11}}\right]}{D}$$

(7) $\partial\psi/\partial x_3 =$

$$-\frac{\partial\phi_3/\partial x_3}{R_{33}}\frac{\left[1 - \dfrac{R_{13}}{R_{11}} - \dfrac{R_{23}}{R_{22}} + \dfrac{R_{21}}{R_{22}}\dfrac{R_{13}}{R_{11}} + \dfrac{R_{12}}{R_{11}}\dfrac{R_{23}}{R_{22}} - \dfrac{R_{21}}{R_{22}}\dfrac{R_{12}}{R_{11}}\right]}{D}$$

where

$$D = 1 - \frac{R_{32}}{R_{31}}\frac{R_{23}}{R_{22}} - \frac{R_{12}}{R_{11}}\frac{R_{21}}{R_{22}} + \frac{R_{12}}{R_{11}}\frac{R_{31}}{R_{33}}\frac{R_{23}}{R_{22}} + \frac{R_{13}}{R_{11}}\frac{R_{21}}{R_{22}}\frac{R_{32}}{R_{33}} - \frac{R_{13}}{R_{11}}\frac{R_{31}}{R_{33}}$$

and $R_{ij} = \partial\phi_{ij}/\partial y_j$

These three conditions together with the production function and the two equations fixing the utility indices of (1) and (2) are sufficient to determine the values of the six variables x_1, x_2, x_3, y_1, y_2, y_3. Any values of the variables satisfying the above three equations and the production function are consistent with our welfare criterion. Subject to the restriction thus imposed, the value of the variables can be determined by an ethical judgment as to the welfare of the individuals.

Let us now consider the economic meaning of these welfare conditions. The left terms $\partial\phi/\partial x_1$, etc., are, of course, the marginal productivities of the services supplied by the three individuals. In the right terms the factor outside the brackets is

$$-(\partial\phi_1/\partial x_1)/(\partial\phi_1/\partial y_1)$$

the familiar marginal rate of substitution for individual (1) between supply of the service x, and income in terms of goods for (1). Thus if the terms in the bracket were equal to (1) we should have the condition that the marginal productivity of a factor has to equal the marginal rate of substitution between leisure and income for every individual supplying the factor. This is one of the welfare conditions already derived for the case in which each individual's utility index *depends only on the size of his individual income*. The terms within the brackets (except for the 1's) are all marginal rates of substitution. The first term, for example, in the equation (5) is

$$-(\partial\phi_2/\partial y_1)/(\partial\phi_2/\partial y_2)$$

This is individual (2)'s marginal rate of substitution between income for himself and income for (1). It is the amount of income required to compensate him for unit change in the income of individual (1). If people are favorably affected by an increase in their neighbors' income, the term is negative. If they are unfavorably affected, it is positive.

The condition can be interpreted in the following way. It is a condition for (3)'s utility being maximized while the utility of the others is fixed. Consequently, if (1) works a little more he must produce just enough additional income to compensate himself for the disutility undergone. The increase in (1)'s income per unit of increased effort must equal his marginal rate of substitution between work and goods. But if (1) is to get more income the others are affected. If they are affected adversely by an increase in income then (1)'s increased effort must not only produce enough to compensate him but must also produce enough to compensate the others for the fact that (1) has obtained more income. The remaining terms in the numerator express the fact that still further adjustments are required to compensate (2) and (3) for the changes in each other's position. The denominator can be regarded as expressing the further adjustment required because (1)'s position is changed by the compensation of (2) and (3) for the changes in each other's position.

Before going further with the interpretation of our welfare conditions it can be noted that our conditions become the ordinary ones if we drop the assumption of interdependence. If each individual's utility depends only on his income, then his marginal rate of substitution between income for himself and income for others is zero. If this is so, all the terms in the brackets except the 1 become zero and we have the usual welfare condition.

The meaning of our conditions can be clarified if we consider a case in which the interdependences are asymmetrical. Suppose that (3)'s utility is dependent on (2)'s income, but not vice versa. Similarly, suppose that (2)'s utility depends on (1)'s income but not vice versa. Then the terms showing (2)'s reaction to changes in (1)'s income and (1)'s reaction to changes in the incomes of (2) and (3) become zero. We then have:

$$\frac{\partial \psi_1}{\partial x_1} = -\frac{\partial \phi_1 / \partial x_1}{R_{11}} \left[1 - \frac{R_{21}}{R_{22}} - \frac{R_{31}}{R_{33}} + \frac{R_{21}}{R_{22}} \frac{R_{32}}{R_{33}} \right]$$

$$\frac{\partial \psi}{\partial x_2} = -\frac{\partial \phi_2 / \partial x_2}{R_{22}} \left[1 - \frac{R_{32}}{R_{33}} \right]$$

$$\frac{\partial \psi}{\partial x_3} = -\frac{\partial \phi_3 / \partial x_3}{R_{33}}$$

At the maximum position a small increment in effort by (3) must produce enough to compensate him. But an increment in effort by (2) must not only compensate (2) but must make up to (3) the loss resulting from (2)'s gain in income. (1)'s efforts must produce enough to compensate both (2) and (3) for his gain in income and to compensate (3) for (2)'s gain in income.

What kind of application does this result have? Suppose we have a community which pays wages equal to marginal productivity. Each individual will take the consumption of the others as a parameter in adjusting his consumption. We will have for the ith individual

$$W_i = \partial\psi/\partial x_i = (\partial\phi_i/\partial x_i)/\partial\phi_i/\partial y_i)$$

so that our welfare conditions are not satisfied. Now suppose that preferences have the kind of interdependence discussed in Chapter III. Low-income groups are affected by the consumption of high-income groups but not vice versa. Further suppose that the individuals have different productivities. Then we shall have the situation described above. The lowest-income group will be affected by the consumption of the next higher group but not vice versa, the lowest but one will be affected by the next higher but not vice versa, and so on.

If we desire to satisfy the welfare conditions while allowing individuals to choose the amount of work they will do, how are we to proceed? If for allocational reasons (which would come into play if more than one good were involved) wage rates are equal to marginal productivities, it is clear that an income tax is required. Moreover, the tax would have to be progressive. The schedule would have to be arranged so that at the equilibrium point the marginal rate on the highest-income group (1) would be

$$1/[1 - R_{21}/R_{22} - R_{31}/R_{33} + (R_{21}/R_{22})(R_{32}/R_{33})].$$

In the middle group the marginal rate would be $1/(1 - R_{32}/R_{33})$. The rate on the lowest group would be zero. However, these conditions will not be sufficient to determine the whole tax schedule.

To do this we have to introduce the equations specifying the welfare levels to be allowed all but one of the participants as well as the production equation. If, for example, it is desired to maintain the welfare levels attained by (1) and (2) before the tax, it would be necessary to repay the proceeds of the income tax in the form of a lump sum bounty.[3] This, however, is not likely to be a problem since most people seem to prefer equality in income distribution in so far as that is compatible with efficiency.

This consideration leads to an important contrast between our results and those of the welfare analyses which neglect interdependence. The latter analyses have indicated that efficiency (that is, the attainment of a conditional maximum for the W function) and equalitarian income distributions can be attained together only by means of devices which are administratively impractical. The maximum welfare conditions require that wages (net of taxes) should equal marginal productivity. It follows that redistributions of income can be made only by means of lump sum taxes and bounties. To produce any change in distribution the taxes would have to be higher for those with high productivity than for those with low productivity. But at the same time they must be levied in such a way as not to influence directly the amount of work done. Professor Samuelson[4] has suggested that this could only be achieved by first finding out what each man's income would be in the absence of taxes. Then a lump sum tax could be levied on each individual. This would be progressive with respect to the calculated or potential income but invariant with respect to actual income. Thus the terms on which income could be traded for work would be independent of the taxes.

Since the system just described is administratively impractical, the conclusion has been reached that inequality can be reduced only at the expense of allocational efficiency.

However, if our assumptions are realistic, the difficulty is at

---

[3] Their incomes would be lower than before the taxes, however. This is so because their willingness to work is reduced by the taxes. They do not therefore end where they start.

[4] Samuelson, *loc. cit.*

least partially solved. We have concluded that progressive income taxes are *necessary* to allocational efficiency. If it is desired to make the distribution more equal (than that resulting from payment of productivity wages) this can be done by distributing the proceeds of the taxes in lump sum bounties or socially consumed services in any way whatever. Of course, the proceeds of the taxes will not be independent of the distribution of the proceeds so that the tax and transfer payment systems would have to be arranged together. Moreover, there are limits to the amount of redistribution which can be obtained by this method. But although there are limits to the amount of redistribution attainable by income taxes consistent with allocational efficiency, it is apparent that a good deal could be accomplished in this way.

Before concluding this section it may be desirable to drop the formal analysis and try to make our results intuitively meaningful. Aside from redistribution what is the nature of the gain from levying income taxes? What is the operational meaning of (1)'s marginal rate of substitution between income for himself and income for (2)? The latter question will lead us into a discussion of some fundamental aspects of the logic of welfare ethics.

In the ordinary case we suppose that under ideal conditions we could determine an individual's preference system by offering him various choices. Once the system is determined the marginal rate of substitution is easily explained in terms of the results of the experiments.

In our case we could offer choices not only between collections of goods but between income for the subject and income for other people. We could ask him for example whether he would rather have his own income increased by 50 per cent while everyone else's increased tenfold, or have his income increased by 10 per cent while others had theirs increased by 10 per cent. It does not seem certain that everyone would prefer the first alternative.

However, we have a certain distrust of verbal results of this sort. We have the feeling that our subjects would be unable to compare the two situations — that they would not know enough about themselves to tell which situation is better. But if we distrust people's ability to judge which situation would most increase their welfare we thereby attach a meaning to welfare independent of their actual choices.

We can now define the utility indices discussed above in either of two ways: (1) in terms of preferences defined by choices between combinations of income for the subject and for other people, or (2) we can define a measure of welfare independent of avowed preferences. Such a measure can be any objective behavior on the part of the people with whose welfare we are concerned, e.g., the number of times they smile or the score they make on a personality inventory.

In either case the utility index used in the argument above has an operational definition just as satisfactory as that used in ordinary welfare economics. The only difference is that one cannot determine the optimum economic arrangements without an empirical investigation of the causes of welfare.

2. The Growth of Demand

As an explanation of phenomena the "orthodox" theory of demand is fairly useful in a good many connections. But when we consider the growth in sales of new products the theory seems to give no help at all. A glance at the figures of consumer-held stocks of products like washing machines and mechanical refrigerators shows a development which can hardly be explained by variations in price or income or by autonomous changes in taste.

In 1925 less than 1 per cent of wired homes were equipped with mechanical refrigerators, but by 1939, 57 per cent were so equipped. In the interim the relative price of refrigerators had fallen by about 30 per cent while per capita income fell sharply and then returned to its pre-depression level. Similar developments occurred in ownership of electric ranges and washing machines and to a lesser extent in the case of vacuum cleaners. It seems impossible to account for these developments by price and income changes.

As for autonomous changes in taste they are of two sorts. Some of the increase in the use of mechanical devices is the consequence of a changed attitude toward housework and a general change in the position of women. But such changes occur very slowly — it is difficult to suppose that so marked a change in attitudes could occur in a fourteen-year period. (As a longer-run matter the increase in the number of women in the labor force and the decrease in the supply of domestic servants might be important. But these factors could not have been very important during the depression.) Autonomous changes in taste can be produced by advertising and other sales efforts. Evaluation of the efficiency of advertising is exceedingly difficult. The advertisers themselves are unable to find a satisfactory way of measuring the number of people who read an ad, let alone the extent of its influence. Manufacturers of electrical appliances made extensive efforts to stimulate sales, particularly during the depression. In the present state of our knowledge, decisions about the role of advertising must remain a matter of judgment. But although no categorical statement is possible, it seems doubtful that advertising accounts for the phenomena before us.

If neither income nor price nor autonomous changes in taste account for the growth of sales (or stocks in the case of durables) of new products, how can we account for it? A self-generating shift in preferences seems to be the answer. We have already shown that every individual's preferences are dependent on the actual purchases of other individuals. If the interdependence involves a lagged shift in preferences a self-generating growth in demand will result. This can be readily shown by means of a simple model.

We shall make some very unrealistic assumptions in order to make the mathematical results simple. But the deviations from reality are not sufficient to change the fundamental character of the results. We assume

(1) All prices are fixed

(2) Aggregate income is fixed

(3) The distribution of income is rectangular, i.e., income receivers are evenly distributed over a range of incomes from o to T.

(4) A new product y is introduced at time o; this product is

of such a character that people buy either one unit per unit of time or none. An indifference map for y against units of a composite product "all other goods" (since prices are fixed, all the goods but y can be treated as a single product) is shown in Figure 1.

(5) The indifference maps of all individuals are the same.

We now have the following situation. Let the price of the new product be P_y at the time of its introduction. If the price is measured in units of the composite good the expenditure line

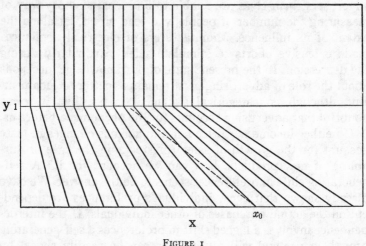

$$y_1$$

$$x$$

$$x_0$$

FIGURE 1

for an individual with income x_0 is a line through the point $y = 0, x = x_0$ with a slope P_y. This is the dotted line in Fig. 1. If the slope P_y is steeper than that of the indifference curve through x_0, the individual with that income will buy one unit of y per unit of time; if the indifference curve is steeper than P_y he will not buy. Now as we go out along the x axis the indifference lines will become progressively flatter — this means that those with higher incomes will give up more other goods for a unit of y than those with low incomes. Starting at the highest income then, the indifference lines will be flatter than P_y. As we pass to lower incomes the indifference lines become steeper. In general there will be some income x_k such that the indifference line through $y = 0$, $x = x_k$ has a slope exactly equal to P_y. Let us call this the critical income. At a price P_y all those with incomes above x_k will buy one unit of y per unit of time. All those with incomes below x_k will refuse to buy.

The whole indifference map can be described by specifying the relation between income and the slope of the indifference line cutting the x axis at that income. That is, by specifying the way in which the indifference lines become flatter as income increases. We can write an equation specifying the income at which the indifference line has a given shape. For simplicity we can make the relation linear so that we have $x = as + b$ when s is the slope. But we know that the critical income is that income corresponding to an indifference curve with slope P_y. Putting $s = P_y$ we may write $x_k = aP_y + b$ when x_k is the critical income.

We have a rectangular income distribution. In the initial situation the sales equal the number of people with income above $aP_y + b$. If the height of the distribution is constant at K and the highest income is T, the total number of buyers is $K[T - (aP_y + b)]$. This will be the rate of sale in the initial period. So far the analysis is just the same as that used in the static demand argument. We now have to consider the effect of interdependent preferences.

Following the argument of Chapter III we assume that preferences for the new product depend on its rate of sale in the period just passed. An increased preference for y is represented by a flattening of the indifference lines. For at each income, people are willing to give up more other goods for a unit of y. Such a result can be represented by changing the parameter a in the relation $x_k = aP_y + b$. If all the indifference lines are flatter the critical income corresponding to a given price is lower. An increase in preference for y can be represented by a reduction in a. If there is a one period lag in the adjustment the value of a at time t depends on the rate of sale y at time $(t-1)$. If we make the relation linear we have

(1) $$a(t) = \alpha Y(t - 1) + \beta.$$

β will represent the initial value of a. But with given preferences, sales are given by

(2) $$Y(t) = K[T - (a(t) P_y + b)].$$

Substituting the value of (a) from equation (1) we have

(3) $$Y(t) = K[T - (\alpha Y(t - 1) + \beta) P_y - b].$$

The static solution (obtained by dropping the time subscripts) is $y = K(T - b - \beta P_y)/(1 + K\alpha P_y)$. This is the level which sales ultimately reach—sometimes called the saturation level of sales for given price and income. The numerator is the initial level of sales (since $\beta =$ the initial value of a). The denominator is less than 1 since α is negative. The final solution is obtained by adding the static solution to the dynamic solution obtained by dropping the constant terms in 3. We have to solve

$$y(t) = -K\alpha P_y\, y(t - 1).$$

Let us put $y_t = ce^{dt}$ then we have $ce^{dt} = -K\alpha P_y \cdot ce^{dt-d}$. Taking logs of both sides

$$\log_e c + dt \log_e e = \log_e(-K\alpha P_y) + \log_e c + (dt - d) \log_e e.$$

Cancelling out we have (since $\log_e e = 1$) $d = \log_e(-K\alpha P_y)$. The constant c can be determined from the initial conditions. At $t = 0$, $y(t - 1) = 0$ and $y(t) = K(T - b - B P_y)$. Adding the static and dynamic relations we have

$$ce^{dt} + K(T - b - \beta P_y)/(1 + K\alpha P_y) = K(T - b - \beta P_y)$$

when $t = 0$ so that

$$c = K\alpha P_y [K(T - b - \beta P_y)/(1 + K\alpha P_y)].$$

Then the final solution is

$$(K\alpha P_y\, e^{t[\log(-K\alpha P_y)]} + 1) K(T - b - \beta P_y)/(1 + K\alpha P_y).$$

If $K\alpha P_y$ is less than 1 in absolute value, $\log(-K\alpha P_y)$ will be negative and the sales will approach the equilibrium value asymptotically. $K\alpha P_y$ is a sort of marginal propensity to consume y with respect to previous sales.[5] It will be less than 1 unless a

[5] A value of $K\alpha P_y$ greater than 1 may easily arise in the first stages but then we should probably run into nonlinearity. In any case a cannot go below zero. When it reaches zero sales are $K(T - b)$ which is the maximum number and the development would stop there.

given increment in sales produces a further increment greater than itself. In general therefore we should expect the growth to follow the pattern of Figure 2.

I = initial sales; E = equilibrium sales

It can now be seen that in spite of our simplified assumptions the results correspond in a general way to the pattern of growth of new products. Saturation at given price and income is not reached immediately but through a process of gradual growth. If we consider only the equilibrium values we get an ordinary demand curve — equilibrium sales as a function of price and income. It will be noted that if price falls as sales grow we will be superimposing one growth curve on another as in Figure 3 in

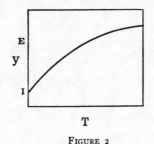

FIGURE 2

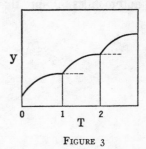

FIGURE 3

which it is assumed that price falls at $t = 1$ and $t = 2$. Changes in income during the development period would cause similar results. Notice that if income fell during the early part of the growth, period sales might continue to increase. This will be the case if sales at the time of a fall in income are below the equilibrium for the *new* level of income. This may explain the growth in sales of some products during a depression.

Finally we note the effect of using a more realistic income distribution. The equilibrium sales would not be changed by introducing a bell-shaped distribution — they depend only on the number of people having more than a certain income. The growth pattern would be changed, however. At first sales would grow more slowly than with a rectangular distribution. But they would grow at an increasing rate because the critical income would be shifted into ranges of income with progressively higher frequencies. Near the mode of the distribution the pattern would be similar to that of a rectangular distribution. But after the critical income falls below the mode (if it does) sales would increase at a slower rate as frequencies fell. The growth pattern therefore, would be not unlike that of a logistic curve.

The idea of shifting preferences seems to explain phenomena which are otherwise difficult to account for. If the analysis is valid it should have a wide range of applications. These include the explanation of sales of new products and the price policy of firms introducing them. There should also be applications in cases of monopolistic competition where consumers' preference for one brand depends largely on the existing sales of the product. It seems probable, for example, that preferences for makes of automobiles fall into this class.

CHAPTER VII

CONCLUSIONS

1. SUMMARY

OUR CONCLUSIONS with regard to saving can be summarized as follows:

(1) In periods of steadily rising income the aggregate savings ratio tends to be independent of income.

(2) The savings ratio will be affected by changes in interest rates, income expectations, the distribution of income, the rate of growth of income, and the age distribution of population.

(3) On balance, changes in these variables have not been sufficiently large to have had much effect on the savings ratio.

(4) Over the trade cycle the savings ratio is dependent on the ratio of current income to previous peak income.

(5) The effect of the two hypotheses taken together can be expressed by the equation $S_t/Y_t = 0.25 \, Y_t/Y_0 - 0.196$, where S_t = current savings, y_t = current disposable income, and y_0 = previous peak disposable income.

(6) The hypotheses just stated are consistent with all the available data.

The theory of saving just summarized is based on the assumption that consumers' preferences are interdependent and irreversible. If the saving theory is satisfactory we have demonstrated the importance of taking interdependence and irreversibility into account. If they are quantitatively important in explaining saving they must be equally important in other branches of consumption theory. A basic reformulation of the theory of consumer behavior is therefore required. Some of the implications of such a reformulation were sketched out in Chapter V but we have hardly scratched the surface of the problem.

Even in the field of saving our work is incomplete. We have concentrated our attention on the income factor because it has generally been considered the most important variable in the determination of saving. But we will not have a complete explanation of saving until we have analyzed in detail a number of other factors. These are (1) the structure of time preference, i.e., the relative importance of present consumption and consumption and asset holdings at various dates in the future, (2) the formation of expectations, (3) the social structure which determines the character of the interdependence of preferences.

2. A Qualification

Our theory of the relation between income and saving really depends on the validity of a single hypothesis, viz.: that the utility index is a function of relative rather than absolute consumption expenditure. In Chapter III we tried to show that psychological considerations make that hypothesis plausible. In Chapter IV we showed that its implications are consistent with observation. But we cannot claim to have proved the hypothesis. Partly for reasons of exposition we have stated the case in a somewhat bald and uncompromising way. Having developed the whole theory we can now try to evaluate its weaknesses and ask what the alternatives are.

The view that preferences are a matter of individual personality alone is certainly untenable. The differences in consumption patterns between societies and the similarities within them require us to regard consumption behavior as a social phenomenon. But the social forces acting on consumers may operate in many ways. There is no question then of proving our hypothesis on logical grounds. What we have tried to do is to show that it does follow from the characteristics of our culture. We should not expect it to apply to other cultures.

Even for our own culture some modification is required. Moreover, the propositions we have tried to establish will still hold good even if we weaken the hypothesis made in Chapter

III. There, we assumed that all of a family's consumption expenditures are strongly influenced by comparisons with other people's consumption behavior. But we cannot deny that some types of consumption may not be much influenced by these considerations. Suppose for the sake of the argument that some appreciable portion of consumption activity is not directly influenced by other people's consumption. Then the strict proportionality between saving and income will not operate. On the usual assumptions about time preference and income we should expect an increase in the savings ratio as income rises.

But unless this effect is quite powerful it will not influence the saving of families in the lower 75 per cent of the income distribution. As we have already indicated, these families operate in a discontinuity on their preference functions. They are only prevented from increasing their expenditures by the very high costs of dissaving.

As far as this group is concerned our hypothesis can be modified without changing our argument about saving. We only need to maintain that interdependence of preferences is sufficiently strong to keep the lower-income groups from escaping the range of discontinuity in their preference functions. If it is that strong it will still be necessary to reformulate the whole theory of consumer behavior to take it into account.

With regard to the upper ranges of the income distribution the case is different. First, moderate changes in the savings ratio of this group will affect the aggregate savings ratio to a much smaller degree. Second, more types of consumption are influenced by competitive considerations in the upper-income groups than in the lower ones. This is so because the upper-income groups are likely to be more status conscious than the lower ones. In the low-income groups medical attention may be an unavoidable necessity to be obtained as cheaply as possible. In higher-income groups people will be influenced in their choices by social considerations. Similarly, expenditures on recreation and on education of children may be socially influenced to a much greater extent in the upper income groups than in the lower ones.

Consequently, we can modify our hypothesis without invalidating our results with regard to saving or our demonstration of the importance of interdependent preferences in the general theory of consumption.

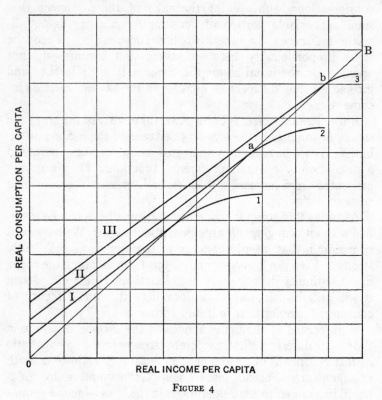

FIGURE 4

3. SAVING AND BUSINESS CYCLE THEORY

Before concluding, it will be worth while to see how our theory fits into the theory of the trade cycle and the theory of economic development. The irreversibility of income consumption relations produces a sort of "ratchet effect." This is illustrated in Figure 4.

The line *OB* is a long-run consumption function shown with a slope of .9. The curves I, II, III, are the short-run functions discussed in Chapter V. The curves marked 1, 2, 3, show the values of consumption in periods when Y_t/Y_0 is substantially above 1. The variations in consumption through a typical business cycle may be described with the aid of the diagram in the following way: suppose that full employment is reached at a certain time with income and consumption at the point a. Full employment is approximately maintained for some years and during this time income and consumption rise approximately proportionately to the point b. When this income is reached a decline in investment occurs so that income is reduced. Consumption now declines but instead of declining proportionately consumption at any income is found at the point corresponding to that income on the curve III. Consumption and income at first fall, then as recovery sets in they advance again. If the recovery is a gradual one, consumption advances along the curve III until the point b is reached once more. After this consumption continues to advance but along the curve OB again until another depression starts. If, however, the recovery is very rapid, then when income passes the level corresponding to b, consumption will increase but along one of the curves 1, 2, or 3, depending on the speed of the increase in income. Income cannot continue, however, to rise at a very rapid rate, for as soon as full employment is reached only increases in productivity will raise income. Eventually, then, a full adjustment to the new living standard will take place and consumption may once more be found by using the line OB.

This "ratchet effect" is an important link between the theory of economic development and trade cycle theory. It explains why each cycle is at a higher level in terms of income and consumption than the preceding one. In each boom, whatever its cause, the gains in productivity since the last boom are exploited. Income rises to a level above the last boom. When investment falls off, income and consumption decline but not to the level of the previous depression. The ratchet keeps the economy from slipping back all the way and losing all the gains in income acquired during the preceding boom. If we had a consumption function based on absolute income, the gap between the income potential of the economy and its actual income would tend to widen as productivity increased. This could only be offset by trend factors in consumption. On our theory, however, the percentage gap between the income at the peak of a boom and income at a zero investment position is fixed by the parameters of our consumption function. We have $S_t/Y_t = 0.25\, Y_t/Y_0 - 0.196$; if net investment is zero, savings must be zero so that $0.25\, Y_t/Y_0 = 0.196$ and $Y_t/Y_0 = 0.78$. Thus, provided investment does not become negative, income will not fall below 78 per cent of the previous peak level.

The economy can absorb increases in productivity provided that a boom of sufficient magnitude occurs periodically. A burst of innovations or a war is capable of doing this. It is not, of course, intended to argue that nothing needs to be done about depressions. But it is important to recognize that the gap between actual and potential income does not need to widen progressively.

BIBLIOGRAPHY

BIBLIOGRAPHY

Books

Bakke, E. W., *The Unemployed Worker* (New Haven: Yale University Press, 1940).

Bowley, A. L., and R. G. D. Allen, *Family Expenditure* (London: P. S. King and Son, Ltd., 1935).

Bowley, A. L., and Josiah Stamp, *Three Studies on the National Income* (reprinted by the London School of Economics and Political Science; University of London, 1938).

Clague, Ewan, and W. J. Couper, *After the Shutdown* (New Haven: Institute of Human Relations, Yale University, 1934).

Clague, Ewan, and W. Powell, *Ten Thousand Out of Work* (Philadelphia: University of Pennsylvania Press, 1933).

Clark, Colin, *National Income and Outlay* (London: Macmillan and Company, Ltd., 1937).

Dubois, Cora, *The People of Alor* (Minneapolis: University of Minnesota Press, 1944).

Frisch, Ragnar, *Statistical Confluence Analysis by Means of Complete Regression Systems* (Oslo: Universetetets okonomiscke, 1934).

Gilboy, Elizabeth W., *Applicants for Work Relief* (Cambridge: Harvard University Press, 1940).

Hansen, Alvin H., *Fiscal Policy and Business Cycles* (New York: W. W. Norton & Company, Inc., 1941).

———, *Economic Policy and Full Employment* (New York: McGraw-Hill Book Company, Inc., 1947).

Harris, Seymour, *Postwar Economic Problems* (New York: McGraw-Hill Book Company, Inc., 1943).

Horney, Karen, *The Neurotic Personality of Our Time* (New York: W. W. Norton & Company, Inc., 1937).

Kalecki, Michal, *Essays in the Theory of Economic Fluctuations* (London: G. Allen & Unwin, Ltd., 1939).

Kardiner, Abram, *The Individual and His Society* (New York: Columbia University Press, 1939).

————, *The Psychological Frontiers of Society* (New York: Columbia University Press, 1940).

Keynes, J. M., *The General Theory of Employment Interest and Money* (New York: Harcourt, Brace & Company, Inc., 1936).

Kuznets, Simon, *Uses of National Income in Peace and War,* Occasional Paper No. 6 (New York: National Bureau of Economic Research, 1942).

Leven, Maurice, H. G. Moulton, and Clark Warburton, *America's Capacity to Consume* (Washington, D. C.: The Brookings Institution, 1934).

Linton, Ralph, *Culture and Personality* (Washington, D. C.: American Council on Education, 1941).

Lough, William H., *High Level Consumption* (New York: McGraw-Hill Book Company, Inc., 1935).

Macaulay, Frederick R., *Bond Yields, Interest Rates and Stock Prices* (New York: National Bureau of Economic Research, 1938).

Marshall, Alfred, *Principles of Economics* (8th ed.; London: Macmillan and Company, Ltd., 1930).

Mendershausen, Horst, *Changes in Income Distribution during the Great Depression* (New York: National Bureau of Economic Research, 1946).

Minnesota Income Study, *Minnesota Incomes 1938–1939, A Report on the Distribution of Family and Individual Incomes,* 4 vols.

National Resources Committee, *Consumer Expenditures in the United States* (Washington, 1938).

National Resources Committee, *Family Expenditures in the United States* (Washington, 1941).

National Resources Committee, *Consumer Incomes in the United States* (Washington, 1939).

Neyman, Jerzy, *Lectures and Conferences on Mathematical Statistics* (Washington: Graduate School of the United States Department of Agriculture, 1938).

Samuelson, Paul A., *Foundations of Economic Analysis* (Cambridge, Mass.: Harvard University Press, 1947).

Shaw, William H., *Finished Commodities Since 1879,* Occasional Paper No. 3 (New York: National Bureau of Economic Research, 1941).

Smith, Adam, *The Wealth of Nations* (New York: The Modern Library, 1937).

Statistical Abstract of the United States (1942).

Tinbergen, J., *Statistical Testing of Business Cycle Theories I, A Method and Its Application to Investment Activity* (Geneva: League of Nations Economic Intelligence Service, 1939).

——, *Statistical Testing of Business Cycle Theories II, Business Cycles in the United States of America, 1919–1932* (Geneva: League of Nations Economic Intelligence Service, 1939).

United States Bureau of Labor Statistics, *Bulletins,* 723, 724, 642–649.

United States Bureau of Home Economics, Miscellaneous Publications 489.

United States Bureau of the Census, *Sixteenth Census, Characteristics of Persons Not in the Labor Force.*

United States Bureau of the Census, *Sixteenth Census, Family Wage or Salary Income in 1939.*

United States Bureau of the Census, *Sixteenth Census, Wage or Salary Income in 1939.*

United States Works Progress Administration, *Workers on Relief in the United States* (March 1935).

Veblen, Thorstein, *The Theory of the Leisure Class* (New York: The Modern Library, 1934).

Warner, W. L., *The Social Life of a Modern Community* (New Haven: Yale University Press, 1941).

——, *The Status System of a Modern Community* (New Haven: Yale University Press, 1942).

Wisconsin Tax Commission, *Wisconsin Income Tax Statistics, Changes in Income of Identical Tax Payers, 1929–35* (Madison: Wisconsin Tax Commission, 1935).

ARTICLES

Bangs, Robert, and Milton Gilbert, "Preliminary Estimates of Gross National Product 1929–1941," *Survey of Current Business* (May 1942).

Bean, Louis, "Relation of Disposable Income and the Business Cycle to Expenditures," *Review of Economic Statistics* (November 1946).

Bennion, E. G., "The Consumption Function: Cyclically Variable?", *Review of Economic Statistics* (November 1946).

Bowley, A. L., "Working Class Expenditure," *Economic Journal* (December 1940).

Brady, Dorothy, "Variations in Family Living Expenditures," *Journal of the American Statistical Association* (June 1938).

————, "Expenditures, Savings and Income," *Review of Economic Statistics* (November 1946).

Bray, J. F. L., "Small Savings," *Economic Journal* (June–September 1940).

Cave, Roy C., "Variations in Consumers Expenditure Where Families Are Classified by Economic Level," *Journal of the American Statistical Association* (December 1943).

Centers, R., and H. Cantril, "Income Satisfaction and Income Aspiration," *Journal of Abnormal and Social Psychology* (January 1946).

Cattell, R. B., "The Concept of Social Status," *Journal of Social Psychology* (May 1942).

Cornfield, J., W. D. Evans, and M. Hoffenburg, "Full Employment Patterns in 1950; Part I," *Monthly Labor Review* (February 1947).

Domar, Evsey, "Capital Expansion, Rate of Growth and Employment," *Econometrica* (April 1946).

Federal Reserve System, Board of Governors of the, "A National Survey of Liquid Assets," *Federal Reserve Bulletin* (July 1946).

Festinger, L., "Wish, Expectation and Group Standards as Factors Influencing Level of Aspiration," *Journal of Abnormal and Social Psychology* (April 1942).

Friend, Irwin, "Relationship Between Consumer Expenditures, Savings and Disposable Income," *Review of Economic Statistics* (November 1946).

Gilboy, E., "Income—Expenditure Relations," *Review of Economic Statistics* (August 1940).

————, "The Propensity to Consume," *Quarterly Journal of Economics* (November 1938).

Haavelmo, Trygve, "The Probability Approach in Econometrics," *Econometrica* (supplement, July 1944).

Hartman, G. W., "The Prestige of Occupations," *Personnel Journal* (October 1934).

Hoffenburg, Marvin, "Estimates of National Output, Distributed Income, Consumer Spending, Saving and Capital Formation," *Review of Economic Statistics* (May 1943).

Johnson, N. O., "The Brookings Report on Inequality in Income," *Quarterly Journal of Economics* (August 1935).

————, "The Pareto Law," *Review of Economic Statistics* (February 1937).

Kaplan, A. D. H., "Expenditure Patterns of Urban Families," *Journal of the American Statistical Association* (March 1938).

Katona, G., and R. Likert, "Relationship Between Consumer Expenditures and Savings: The Contribution of Survey Research," *Review of Economic Statistics* (November 1946).

Keynes, J. M., "The Statistical Testing of Business Cycle Theories," *Economic Journal* (September 1939).

Klein, Lawrence, "Macroeconomics and the Theory of Rational Behaviour," *Econometrica* (April 1946).

———, "A Postmortem on Transitional Predictions of National Product," *Journal of Political Economy* (August 1946).

Koopmans, Tjalling, "The Logic of Econometric Business Cycle Research," *Journal of Political Economy* (April 1941).

Lewis, Cleona, "Trend of Savings, 1900–29," *Journal of Political Economy* (August 1935).

Madge, C., "The Propensity to Save in Blackburn and Bristol," *Economic Journal* (December 1940).

Marschak, J., "Income Inequality and Demand Studies," *Econometrica* (April 1943).

———, "Personal and Collective Budget Functions," *Review of Economic Statistics* (November 1939).

Mendershausen, Horst, "Differences in Family Savings between Cities of Different Sizes and Location, Whites and Negroes," *Review of Economic Statistics* (August 1940).

Monroe, Day, "Analyzing Families by Composition Type with Respect to Consumption," *Journal of the American Statistical Association* (March 1937).

Mosak, J., "Forecasting Postwar Demand, III," *Econometrica* (January 1945).

Painter, Mary S., "Estimates of Gross National Product, 1919–1928," *Federal Reserve Bulletin* (September 1945).

Pollak, J. J., "Fluctuations in United States Consumption, 1919–1932," *Review of Economic Statistics* (February 1939).

Schoenburg, Erika, and Mildred Parten, "Methods and Problems of Sampling Presented by the Urban Study of Consumer Purchases," *Journal of the American Statistical Association* (June 1937).

Shaw, William H., "Consumption Expenditures, 1929–1943," *Survey of Current Business* (June 1944).

Slutzky, Eugen, "The Summation of Random Causes as the Source of Cyclic Processes," *Econometrica* (April 1937).

Smithies, A., "Forecasting Postwar Demand," *Econometrica* (January 1945).

Staehle, Hans, "Retail Sales and Labor Income," *Review of Economic Statistics* (August 1938).

Stone, R. and W. M., "The Marginal Propensity to Consume and the Multiplier, A Statistical Investigation," *Review of Economic Studies* (October 1938).

Tinbergen, J., "Does Consumption Lag Behind Incomes," *Review of Economic Statistics* (February 1942).

————, On a Method of Statistical Research, A Reply," *Economic Journal* (March 1940).

Tucker, Donald S., "The Interest Rate and Saving," *Journal of the American Statistical Association* (March 1943).

Tucker, Rufus, "Distribution of Incomes," *Quarterly Journal of Economics* (August 1938).

————, "Distribution of Income in 1935–36," *Journal of the American Statistical Association* (December 1942).

————, "Estimates of Savings of American Families," *Review of Economic Statistics* (February 1942).

Wallis, W. Allen, "Temporal Stability of Consumption Patterns," *Review of Economic Statistics* (November 1942).

Warburton, Clark, "The Trend of Savings 1900–1929," *Journal of Political Economy* (February 1935).

Williams, Faith, "Methods of Measuring Variations in Family Expenditures," *Journal of the American Statistical Association* (March 1937).

Working, Holbrook, "Statistical Laws of Family Expenditure," *Journal of the American Statistical Association* (March 1943).

Woytinski, W. S., "Relationship between Consumers' Expenditures, Savings and Disposable Income," *Review of Economic Statistics* (January 1946).

Yule, G. Udny, "Why Do We Sometimes Get Nonsense Correlations, A Study in Sampling and the Nature of Time Series," *Journal of the Royal Statistical Society* (January 1926).

INDEX

INDEX

Advertising and demand for new products, 105
Aggregation, theory of, 71–73
Assets and saving, 33–36, 91; valuation of, 36n, 43

Bakke, E. W., 77n
Barone, E., 93

Cattell, R. B., 30n
Centers, R., 48n
Clague, E., 77n
Conspicuous consumption, 28
Consumer behavior theory, 8, 17–46, 93
Consumer Purchases Study, 50–53, 62
Consumer deficits, 77–86; and changes in income, 83–84; and new products, 79–80; and past income, 82; and unemployment, 78, 80–82
Consumption and emulation, 14; and habits, 24–26; and income, 36–38, 40, 69–76; and social mobility, 30; and social status, 29–31; and standard of living, 29–31
Consumption decisions, 22–25
Consumption function, cyclical variations in, 76–89; regressions, 69–76; reversibility of, 2–3; shifts in, 1–3, 57
Consumption, motivations for, 25–32; social role of, 28
Cowles, Alfred, 66

Demand functions, estimation of, 10; reversibility of, 4
Dissaving, 40–43, 64, 77–86
Dubois, Cora, 29n
Durable goods, 60–61

Emulation, 14
Expectations and saving, 10, 33, 36, 39, 40, 45, 57, 65, 92, 111

Festinger, L., 28n
Forecasts, postwar, 69–70

Gilboy, E., 53n, 77 and n

Haavelmo, T., 73n
Habits, consumption, 24–26
Hansen, A., 76 and n
Hartman, G., 30n
Hicks, J., 1
Horney, K., 28n
Hotelling, H., 93
Hypothesis testing, 47, 69–76

Income and consumption, 36–38, 40; and saving, 3, 36–38, 40, 45, 52–58, 69–79
Income aspiration, 48–49
Income distribution and savings, 36, 44–45, 91, 111
Income, past and saving, 76–89
Income taxes and welfare, 102–103
Interest rate and saving, 33, 35–37, 39, 40, 45, 57, 111
Invariant relationships, 71–74

Jevons, W. S., 14
Johnson, N. O., 64n

Kardiner, A., 31n
Knight, F., 14–15
Kuznets, S., 1–3, 55 and n, 56, 59 and n, 60, 65, 71, 90

Lerner, A. P., 93
Life insurance and saving, 67–68
Lorenze curves, 36

Macaulay, F. R., 66
Marshall, Alfred, 10, 14
Mendershausen, Horst, 50n
Mosak, J., 70n
Motivation for saving, 33–34, 41, 67

National Resources Committee, 62n

Negro savings, 50–52

New products, and advertising, 105; and consumer deficits, 79–80; and saving, 4, 57–60; demand for, 4, 57–60, 104–110

Pareto, V., 71, 93

Past income, and consumer deficits, 82; and saving, 4, 76–89

Pigou, A. C., 14n

Population growth and saving, 36, 41–43, 45, 57, 63–64

Powell, W., 77 and n

Preferences, empirical basis for, 9–13; inconsistency in, 11; independence of, 2, 13, 96; interdependence of, 3, 14–17, 34–37, 96–110; randomness of, 12; shifts in, 14, 17–18, 40

Ratchet effect, 115

Samuelson, P. A., 9 and n, 76 and n, 94n, 102n

Savings, and assets, 91, 33–36; and expectations, 10, 33, 36, 39–40, 45, 57, 65, 92, 111; and income, 3, 36–38, 40, 45, 52–58, 111; and income distribution, 36, 44–45, 91, 111; and interest rate, 33, 35–37, 39–40, 45, 57, 111; and life insurance, 67–68; and new products, 4, 57–60; and past income, 76–89; and population,

36, 45, 57, 63–64; and urbanization, 3, 57, 61–62; by Negroes, 50–52; motivation for, 33–34, 41, 67; trends in, 56–69

Self-esteem, 29–31

Shaw, W. H., 59 and n

Smithies, A., 57 and n, 70n

Social mobility, 30

Social status, 29–31, 48

Standard of living, 26, 29–31

Statistical estimation, 5

Tastes, changes in, 14, 17–18

Time preference, 33, 39–40, 45, 57, 67–68, 112

Trends in savings, 56–69

Unemployment and dissaving, 78, 80–82

Urbanization and saving, 3, 57, 61–62

Utility theory, 9, 13–15, 93–94; index, 9–10, 32–35

Veblen, T., 14–15

Warner, W. L., 30n

Welfare economics, 4, 93–104; and ethics, 93–95; and income taxes, 102–103; and interdependent preferences, 96–104; and measurement of welfare, 103–104

Woytinski, W. S., 76 and n

Galaxy Books

ECONOMICS

A. N. AGARWALA & S. P. SINGH, Eds.: The Economics of Underdevelopment   GB97

EDUARD HEIMANN: History of Economic Doctrines: An Introduction to Economic Theory   GB123

CLARK KERR, JOHN T. DUNLOP, FREDERICK H. HARBISON & CHARLES A. MYERS: Industrialism and Industrial Man. Second edition   GB107

JOSEPH A. SCHUMPETER: Ten Great Economists: From Marx to Keynes   GB140

JOSEPH A. SCHUMPETER: The Theory of Economic Development. Translated by Redvers Opie   GB55

HISTORY

DANIEL AARON: Men of Good Hope: A Story of American Progressives   GB58

T. S. ASHTON: The Industrial Revolution, 1760–1830   GB109

CARL & JESSICA BRIDENBAUGH: Rebels and Gentlemen: Philadelphia in the Age of Franklin   GB141

GEOFFREY BRUUN: Nineteenth Century European Civilization, 1815–1914   GB36

GEORGE CLARK: Early Modern Europe: From About 1450 to About 1720   GB37

GEORGE CLARK: The Seventeenth Century. Second edition   GB47

R. G. COLLINGWOOD: The Idea of History   GB1

GORDON A. CRAIG: The Politics of the Prussian Army, 1640–1945   GB118

SIR ALAN GARDINER: Egypt of the Pharaohs   GB165

WERNER JAEGER: Paideia: The Ideals of Greek Culture. Volume I: Archaic Greece: The Mind of Athens. Translated by Gilbert Highet   GB144

ADRIENNE KOCH: Jefferson and Madison: The Great Collaboration   GB110

SAMUEL ELIOT MORISON: Sources and Documents Illustrating the American Revolution, 1764–1788, and the Formation of the Federal Constitution   GB135

H. ST. L. B. MOSS: The Birth of the Middle Ages, 395–814   GB130

HERBERT J. MULLER: The Loom of History   GB170

HERBERT J. MULLER: The Uses of the Past: Profiles of Former Societies   GB9

MERRILL D. PETERSON: The Jefferson Image in the American Mind   GB71

M. ROSTOVTZEFF: Greece. Edited by Elias J. Bickerman   GB98

M. ROSTOVTZEFF: Rome. Translated by J. D. Duff. Edited by Elias J. Bickerman   GB42

J. M. THOMPSON: The French Revolution   GB172

DAVID THOMSON: World History, 1914–1961   GB116

THUCYDIDES: The History of the Peloponnesian War. Edited in translation by Richard W. Livingstone   GB33

ARNOLD J. TOYNBEE: A Study of History
   Volume I: Introduction; The Geneses of Civilizations, Part One   GB74
   Volume II: The Geneses of Civilizations, Part Two   GB75
   Volume III: The Growths of Civilizations   GB76
   Volume IV: The Breakdowns of Civilizations   GB77
   Volume V: The Disintegrations of Civilizations, Part One   GB78
   Volume VI: The Disintegrations of Civilizations, Part Two   GB79
   Volume VIIA: Universal States   GB80
   Volume VIIB: Universal Churches   GB81
   Volume VIII: Section 1: Heroic Ages
   Section 2: Contacts Between Civilizations in Space   GB82
   Volume IX: Section 1: Contacts Between Civilizations in Time
   Section 2: Law and Freedom in History
   Section 3: The Prospects of Western Civilization   GB83
   Volume X: The Inspirations of Historians   GB84
   Volume XII: Reconsiderations   GB85

G. M. TREVELYAN: The English Revolution, 1688–1689   GB146

A. S. TURBERVILLE: English Men and Manners in the Eighteenth Century: An Illustrated Narrative — GB10

JOHN WILLIAM WARD: Andrew Jackson: Symbol for an Age — GB73

LYNN WHITE, JR.: Medieval Technology and Social Change — GB163

C. VANN WOODWARD: The Strange Career of Jim Crow. Second revised edition — GB6

C. VANN WOODWARD: Tom Watson: Agrarian Rebel — GB102

G. M. YOUNG: Victorian England: Portrait of an Age. Second edition — GB129

ALFRED E. ZIMMERN: The Greek Commonwealth: Politics and Economics in Fifth-Century Athens. Fifth edition, revised — GB62

POLITICAL SCIENCE

ARISTOTLE: The Politics. Edited and translated by Sir Ernest Barker — GB69

SIR ERNEST BARKER, Ed.: Social Contract: Essays by Locke, Hume, and Rousseau — GB68

ISAIAH BERLIN: Karl Marx: His Life and Environment. Third edition — GB25

JOHN BOWLE: Politics and Opinion in the Nineteenth Century — GB119

JOSEPH FRANKEL: International Relations — GB117

A. D. LINDSAY: The Modern Democratic State — GB86

RICHARD LOWENTHAL: World Communism: The Disintegration of a Secular Faith — GB156

ALEXANDER MEIKLEJOHN: Political Freedom: The Constitutional Powers of the People — GB145

H. G. NICHOLAS: The United Nations as a Political Institution. Second edition — GB105

SIR HAROLD NICOLSON: Diplomacy — GB115

DEXTER PERKINS: The Evolution of American Foreign Policy. Second edition — GB159

DON K. PRICE: Government and Science — GB72

THOMAS C. SCHELLING: The Strategy of Conflict — GB101

K. C. WHEARE: Federal Government — GB112

K. C. WHEARE: Legislatures — GB104